Electronic Components Failure Analysis: Methods and Experience for Beginners

By

Steve Sung

Electronic Components Failure Analysis: Methods and Experience for Beginners

Author: Steve Sung

Published by: SUNG TSAI FENG

Publisher Address:
No. 18, Ln. 31, Sec. 1, Huaxing Rd.,Dayuan Dist., Taoyuan City 337009,Taiwan (R.O.C.)

Tel: +886 935 232 110

Publication Date: December 2025

Edition: 1.0

ISBN: 978-626-01-5418-9

This book is based on real-world experience working in an electronics factory, covering topics not taught in school curricula. When an electronic product malfunctions, the key is to identify the root cause to prevent recurring defects in mass production, aiming to improve yield.

However, investigating malfunctions can be customer-related or product-related. Simply replacing the faulty component isn't enough. Companies like Apple, Sony, and Toshiba require an 8D report (Eight Disciplines Problem Solving). This necessitates using the instruments and analytical data described in the book to prove the true cause of the defect and conduct more Design of Experiments (DOEs) to demonstrate the effectiveness of improvements. Without this analytical knowledge, the job will be difficult.

It's essential for high school freshmen, university students, quality control personnel, and electronics industry professionals to learn this knowledge. Without relevant experience, you won't have seen it before, won't know how to do it, and might not even recognize the images in the book. The knowledge and practical analytical reports presented are extremely valuable. Reading this book can save you a year of study time, allowing you to surpass others in your work. Investing in this book is worthwhile.

Electronic Components Failure Analysis: Methods and Experience

Electronic Components Failure Analysis: Methods and Experience

When I wanted to work in the enviable electronics industry, I was assigned to the quality control department by chance, which seemed cool to everyone, but I found it a tough job . As an unprepared rookie, I entered the quality control department, and I had to pass on the experience of solving problems one after another.

This article teaches what is not taught in school, and uses various case studies to understand the analysis report and analysis techniques, hoping to improve the beginner's skills.
Are you ready? Starting to take you into the world of electronic factory quality problems Debug, together jump into the Red Ocean of competition in the electronics industry!

Chapter 1: BGA IC Soldering Failure

BGA Start

There are hundreds of small solder balls in the BGA package, all of them are located at the lower end of the IC, the soldering situation cannot be seen and it is difficult to control the quality of the product. One day the market
responded that the product would out of order. Sometimes the product would go back to normal by pressing the IC, and the product was held in the dealership. The QC is responsible for handling the situation

Exit of Changzhou Railway Station, China, the square is very big and busy.

Each chapter is an independent case, the beginning of the red ink staining analysis is a bit complicated, it is recommended to choose a simpler chapter to start reading,
For example, the second chapter is simpler, wait until you have some experience and then go back to read the first chapter.

Shanghai Pudong Airport

Oriental Pearl Tower at the mouth of the Huangpu River in Shangha

DYE and PRY test : [Classification: Destructive analysis]

The defective product was confirmed to be a problem with BGA IC welding, and the cause of the failure was investigated. The BGA ball pitch of 0.5 mm is as small as the tip of a ball pen. If you want to know the distribution of BGA solder ball fractures and whether the solder ball welding fracture surface is located at the IC end or the substrate end, the best way to perform failure analysis is to dye with red ink.

That is, in a vacuum environment, the red ink is infiltrated into the welding of the fine seams between the parts, and the cracks and fracture distribution areas of the solder ball welding are checked to find out the causes of circuit failure such as cold welding or external stress fracture.

Figure 1-1 is a Red Dye Penetration Test report, with Type 1, 2, 3, and 4 colors indicating the location of the fracture. For example, the yellow arrow (Type 3) indicates a crack between the BGA solder ball and the PCB copper pad. Type A, B, C, and D and the size of the red area indicate the degree of fracture. For example, Type D has the most red ink penetration, with a fracture degree of 76-100%. Finally, a matrix grid is used to fill in the analysis results, with each grid representing a solder ball. The advantage of red ink dye analysis is that the defect distribution status of the entire IC can be seen at once, unlike the cross-section analysis that can only see the status of a tangent line. The disadvantage of the red ink analysis method is that the cause of the fracture point cannot be seen in detail.

Usually, stress damage to BGA will occur at the four corners of IC, because the four corners are the maximum stress points of the stress path. When designing, IC manufacturers will avoid installing solder balls at the four corners or skillfully install solder balls without electrical functions. Note! Red ink dyeing analysis is a destructive analysis method. It must be reported to the customer first. The product cannot be restored to its original state after testing. Failure to report means that you want to drown the evidence. Destroying evidence will be blamed by the customer. Please consider other non-destructive methods such as X-Ray and ultrasonic inspection first. There is a Type D light blue grid in the lower right corner of the case inspection result. Light blue means that the fracture is at the BGA pad and the BGA solder ball end. Type D means that the fracture is 76-100%, which is usually caused by the user end and is not the responsibility of the IC manufacturer. It also occurs at the corner 8H position, and it is likely to be damaged by external stress.

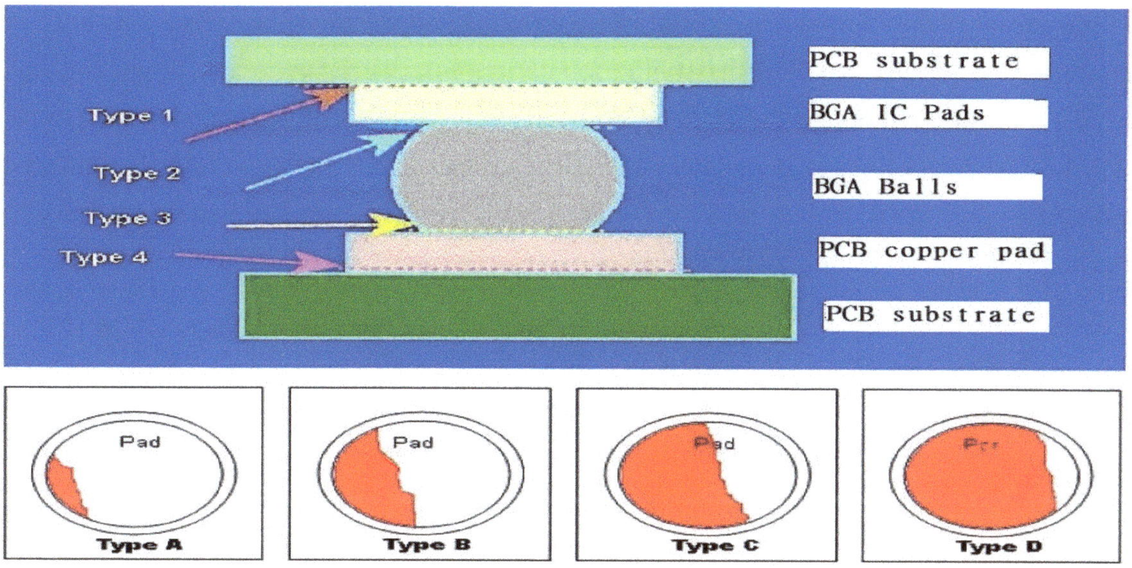

Type 0 = No cracks observed
Type A = Crack size percentage between 1 – 25%
Type B = Crack size percentage between 26 – 50%
Type C = Crack size percentage between 51 – 75%
Type D = Crack size percentage between 76 – 100%

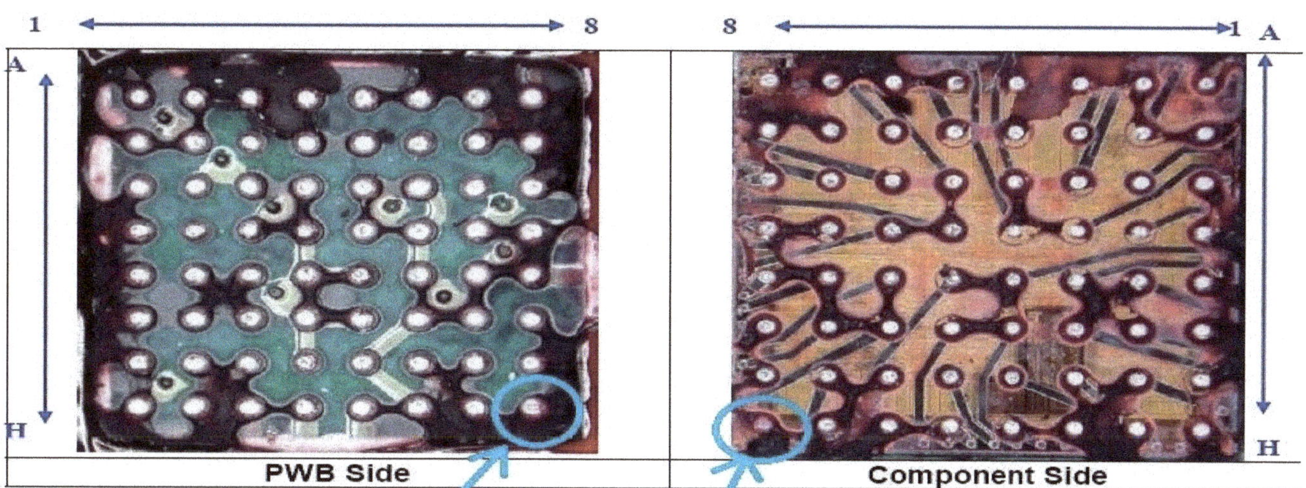

Solder balls stick to the PWB side

Point 8H has been penetrated by 76~100% of red ink, located at the BGA IC pad (Type 2)

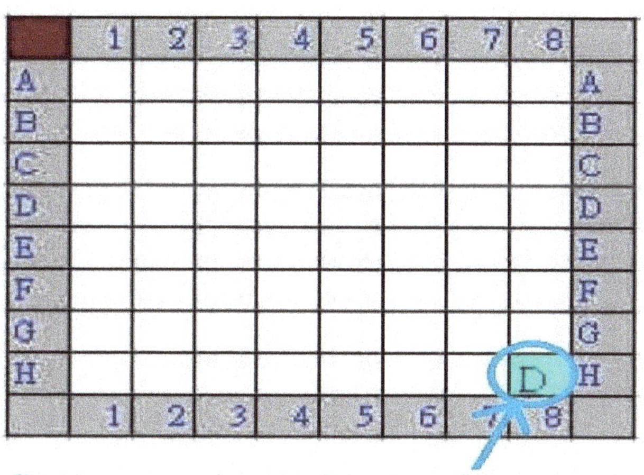

Corners are points of maximum external stress

Fracture Type	Number	% Total
No fracture	63	98.4
Type1	0	0.0
Type2	1	1.6
Type3	0	0.0
Type4	0	0.0
Total	64	100

Crack Size	Number	% Total
Type 0	63	98.4
Type A	0	0.0
Type B	0	0.0
Type C	0	0.0
Type D	1	1.6
Total	64	100

Figure 1-1. Red Dye Penetration Test report (8H position is bad, color is light blue, letter D)

The possible causes and recommended countermeasures related to stress damage are as follows:

1. The circuit board softens and deforms at high temperature in the reflow oven. When cooling, the solder paste solidifies first, and the PCB board bends at high temperature and slowly returns to its original state when cooling. This recovery stress causes the solder paste to crack. Countermeasure: Using a carrier during reflow can prevent the PCB from softening and deforming, thereby suppressing this type of solder cracking defect.

2. The cooling slope of the reflow is insufficient, and the metal tin in the solder ball gathers and solidifies first, forming a phenomenon of enlarged crystal particles, resulting in insufficient strength. The cooling slope of the profile can be readjusted to more than -3 °C/second (subject to experimentation) to allow the tin to quickly enter the solid phase from the liquid phase, so that the alloy components have no extra time to condense each other, achieving the purpose of fine crystal particle structure and enhanced strength. If the cooling slope is fast and rapid cooling, the crystal particles will be small, and the solder ball will have a bright appearance and color. Cheap reflow equipment is mostly air-cooled, with poor rapid cooling capabilities. Water-cooled cooling systems are a good choice, but they are more expensive.

3. The PCB material is not good. When the PCB is exposed to high temperature, it softens and produces a large deformation. Review whether the heating pre-stressing and stress relief time of the last process in the PCB manufacturing process is extended or replace the PCB with a high Tg material (Tg, glass transition temperature), for example, Tg 135 is replaced with Tg 150.

4. The stress of separating boards and dropping will cause tin cracks. BGA solder balls are small and are easily cracked by external forces. Operators use manual separation for convenience. Manual separation is strictly prohibited to prevent the possibility of PCB stress. Design also includes arranging parts away from the maximum stress point on the board edge, and horizontal or vertical placement of parts also has an impact.

It is recommended to retrieve the actual object after reading the lab report and then view it yourself under a microscope. The angle of the oblique angle can more clearly see which side the solder ball is attached to.
Since the PCB pad design area is larger than the IC solder ball, the solder ball usually remains on the PCB.

There is also information about the shape of the fracture. In the enlarged picture of the solder ball in the following chapter, whether the cross section is serrated or arc-shaped, the serrated shape is the solder that is pulled apart after welding, so it is the correct way to take the actual object back and view it yourself.
The new version of the red ink test adds a solder ball middle fracture, the principle is the same, and the Type type is increased by 1 to Type 5.

2D/3D X-ray analysis : [Classification: Non-destructive analysis]

The leads of BGA, QFN (Quad Flat No Lead), FBP (Flat Bump Package) and other parts are hidden at the bottom of the parts. Cold soldering and Solder balls cracks cannot be detected by visual inspection. Poor quality is poor quality. Customers must use it 100% and don't expect to get away with it.
Note: Thermal testing can detect more defective products, such as setting the oven at 90~100°C and testing the board after 30 minutes.

Checking the soldering conditions, such as whether the gold wire inside the LED is broken or the bubbles in the BGA solder, requires X-ray to see inside the component. X-ray inspection can easily check the internal conditions of an object, but the disadvantage is that the micro cracks of a few μm cannot be judged from the image due to the resolution.

3D X-Ray inspection examples are shown in Figure 1-2. In order to determine whether the BGA IC has Head-in-Pillow, the camera angle needs to be rotated during inspection to capture the 3D shape for easy judgment. In Figure 1-2, double circular shadows are seen at the arrows. The solder ball and the printed solder paste have not merged into one ball.

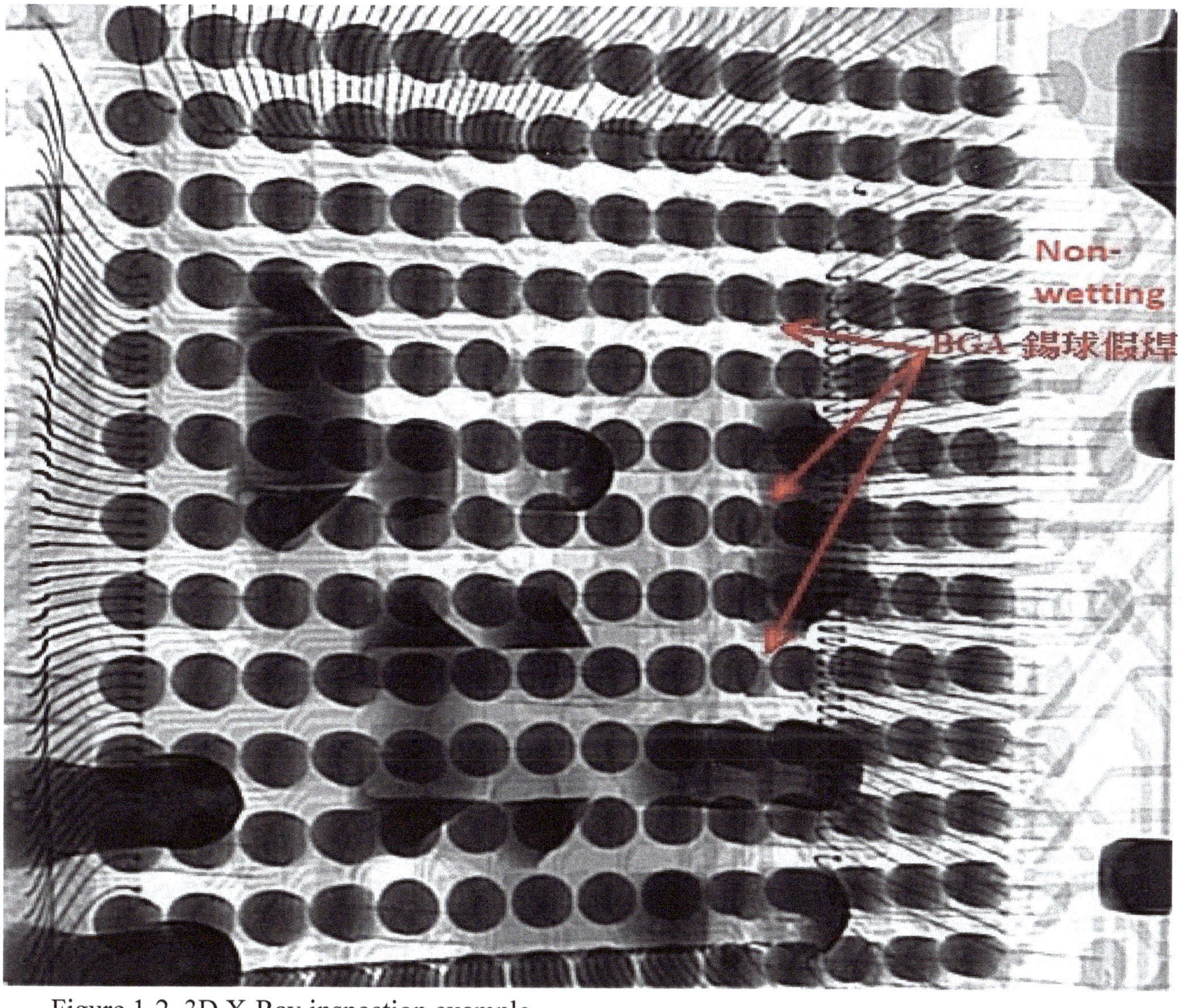

Figure 1-2. 3D X-Ray inspection example

It is obvious that the soldering is poor. There are multiple rows of solder balls on the right side of the picture that have Head-in-Pillow defects. First, a few causes are briefly listed. Future articles will discuss Head-in-Pillow in more detail.

1. The reflow oven temperature is insufficient; the furnace temperature is not measured before production; special IC high temperature requirements
2. Whether the solder paste is oxidized after being stopped on the production line for too long (occurs when the machine is repaired).
3. Whether the solder paste is stirred and placed in the refrigerator for too long and deteriorates.
4. Inaccurate amount of Insufficient solder paste
5. Whether the IC solder ball is oxidized (IC humidity management check).
6. IC solder ball composition and solder paste wettability
7. Nitrogen processing reduces oxidation.

Figure 1-3 uses X-Ray to check the size of the voids in the solder ball. The light white dots in the black sphere are voids. If the voids exceed 25%, it will affect the soldering strength. Customers will regard it as poor process technology. The profile must be adjusted, such as increasing the heating temperature and preheating time to allow sufficient time for the flux to escape from the solder paste to solve the voids phenomenon, increase soldering strength, and improve product reliability.

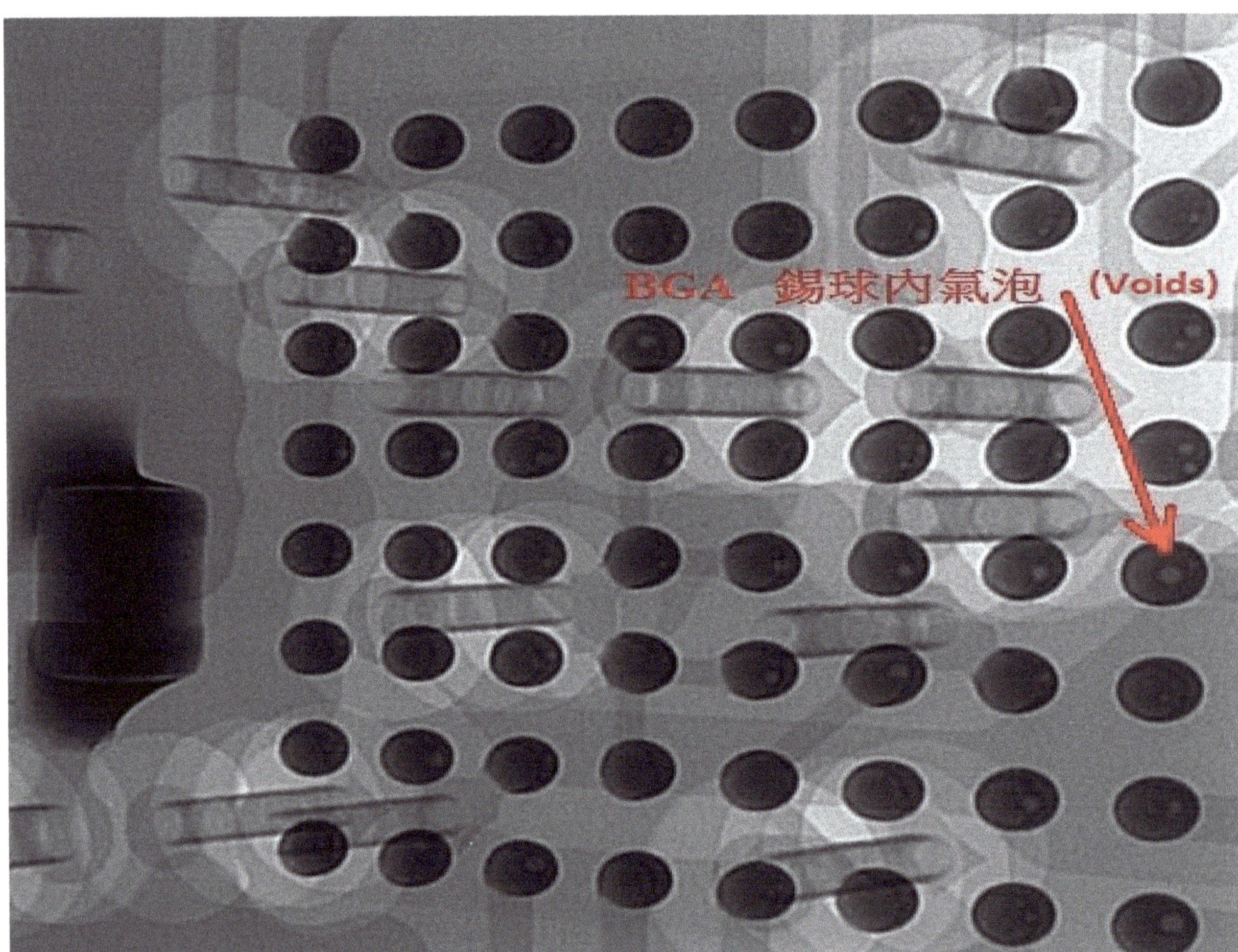

Figure 1-3. X-Ray inspection of voids size

Cross-Sectioning analysis : [Classification: Destructive analysis]

In order to find out the detailed reasons for poor BGA soldering, you can entrust a verification company to conduct a cross-section analysis . Cross-section analysis is a destructive analysis. The material needs to go through cold embedding (acrylic adhesive fixing treatment), cutting and polishing and grinding steps, and then observe the cross section with an optical microscope or electron microscope. The two have different magnifications and prices, and electron microscopes are more expensive.
Figures 1-4 and 1-5 are BGA solder ball cross-section . Figure 1-4 shows that there is a fracture between the upper end of the solder ball and the IC pad. The shape of the fracture has tear marks, and the shapes of the upper and lower ends match, which means that the solder ball was broken by stress after cooling. Furthermore, electron microscopes can be used to measure the thickness of the IMC (Intermetallic Compound) layer generated at the welding position. The thickness of the alloy composition IMC layer contains a lot of important information. The best thickness is 1~3u. Too thick or too thin is not good. Cross-section analysis can obtain such rich information. No wonder everyone likes to use cross-section analysis . Some electronics manufacturers such as DELL require cross-section analysis reports for BGA initial process and rework.

Figure 1-4. Cross-section of a BGA IC with a fracture

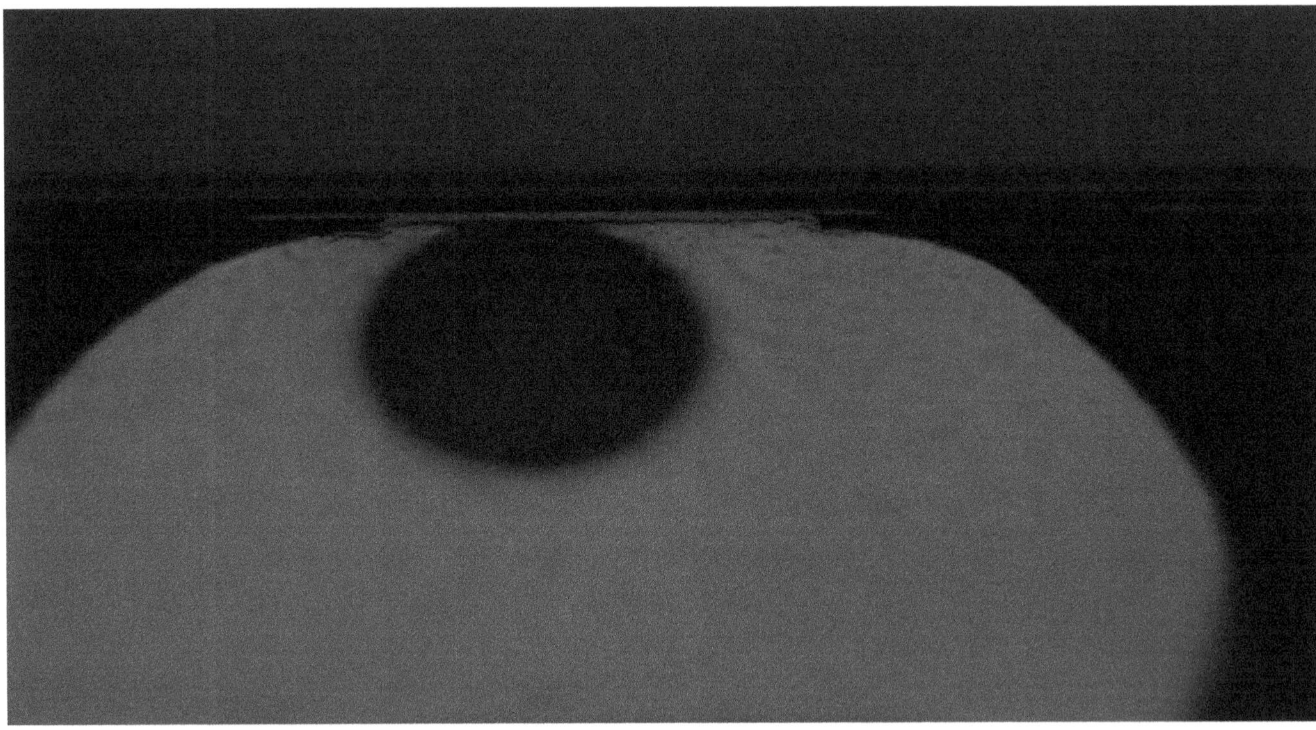

Figure 1-5. Cross-section of BGA IC substrate with voids(bubbles) between pads

Figure 1-6 illustrates another poor soldering phenomenon. The picture clearly shows that the BGA solder ball and the printed solder paste below are not mutually melted. Since the contact surface between the solder ball and the solder paste is smooth, it proves that it is not damaged by external force. If force is applied to the solidified solder paste, the fracture surface must be torn and broken. The sliced picture shows that this defect has already occurred in the reflow oven, and the responsibility for the defect belongs to the SMT unit.

Figure 1-6. BGA solder ball and printed solder paste do not melt together. (Head-in-Pillow) (The reason here is insufficient temperature)

The possible causes of Head-in-Pillow and the recommended countermeasures are as follows:

1. The solder balls are oxidized when BGA materials are received or the materials are not properly stored and contaminated or oxidized. The supplier needs to analyze and review the IC storage equipment in the factory.

2. The heating time of the solder furnace profile is insufficient. Review the components and solder paste ingredients. For example, the tin plating of components sometimes requires higher temperature and heating time.

3. Profile preheating time is too long, causing the flux in the solder paste to volatilize too quickly, failing to achieve the purpose of cleaning oxides. This phenomenon is especially obvious on smaller BGA solder balls. Contrary to the general perception that the longer the time, the better, you can try to shorten the preheating time.

4. Improper storage of solder paste, exceeding the validity period after unpacking or uneven mixing, and the production line is stopped for too long after solder paste printing. When the reflow or machine equipment fails, the line is stopped for too long. The solder paste on the PCB board or the solder paste in the solder paste printer is not properly collected and sealed for storage, and is exposed to the environment for too long, causing the flux in the solder paste to evaporate completely, and lack the ability to clean oxides.

5. If the solder paste flux cleaning ability is insufficient, you can try another brand of solder paste, such as ALMIT, Japan Senju, etc. Good solder paste can be wetted within 10 seconds when it is molten, while poor solder paste takes more than 30 seconds. The fastest solution is to find the supplier for review.

6. There are also cases where the IC tilts or the PCB deforms during the soldering process in the reflow oven, causing some soldered terminals to float and separate from the solder paste. They only come down and touch the solder paste when they start to cool, but it is too late because the temperature is not high enough.

7. You can replace a batch of materials and conduct cross-tests to see if the problem is with the IC material.

8. Blockage of the holes in the printed steel plate will lead to insufficient solder paste, resulting in the inability of the solder balls to touch each other and forming a pillow phenomenon.

9. Consider adding nitrogen (N2) processing, because when the furnace is under high temperature, all metal materials are prone to oxidation. Nitrogen can isolate oxygen and slow down the oxidation phenomenon. The effect is equivalent to raising the furnace temperature by 10°C, which is very helpful for improving welding.

Abnormal example

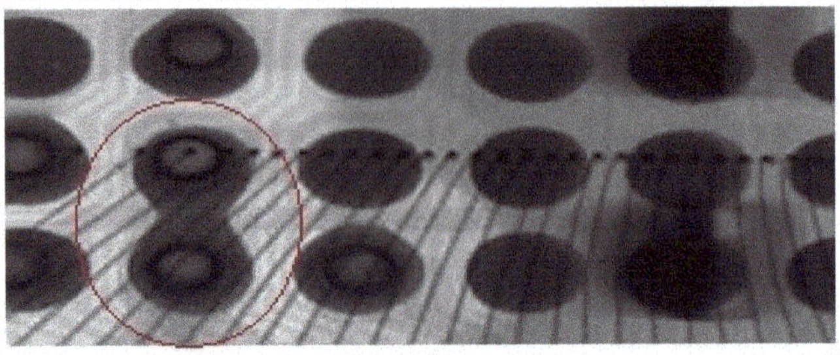	Solder Bridging 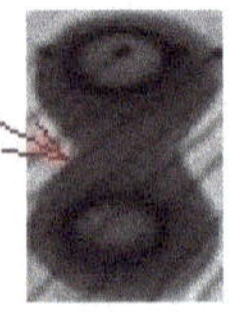
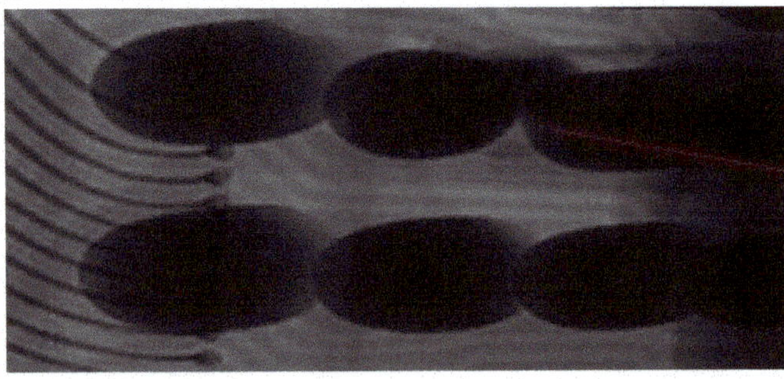	Green solder mask overflow 
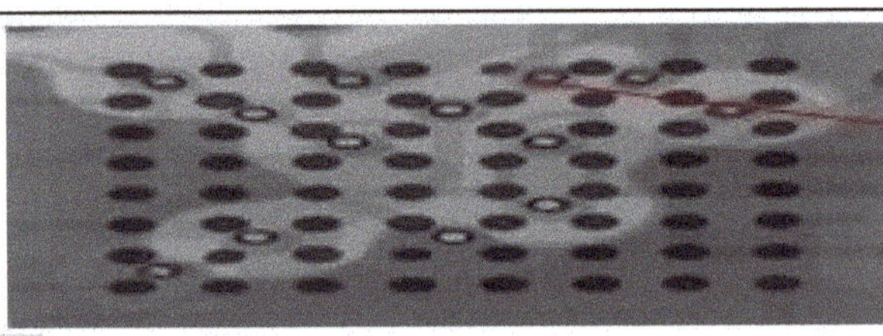	Insufficient solder paste 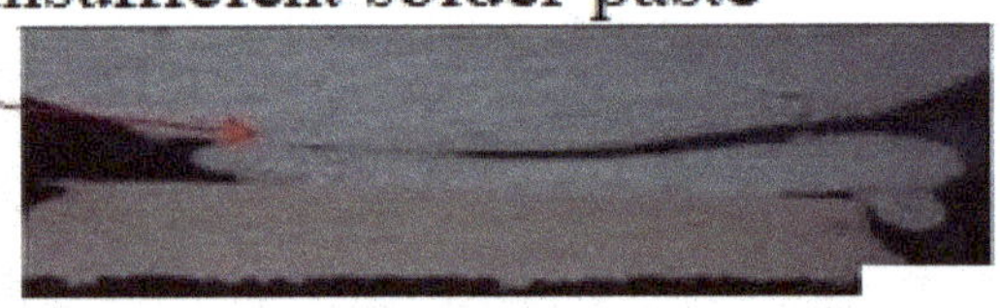
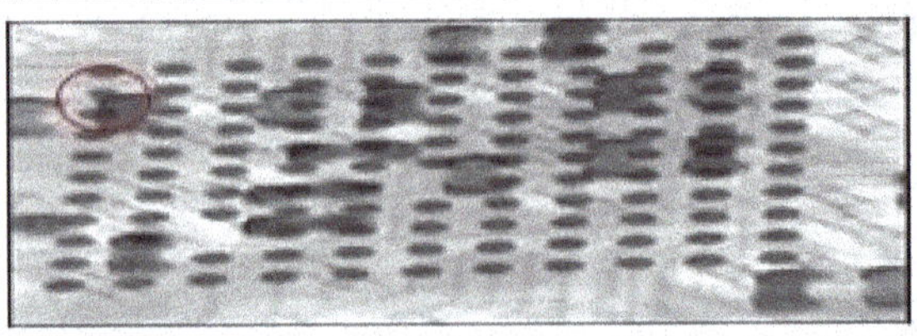	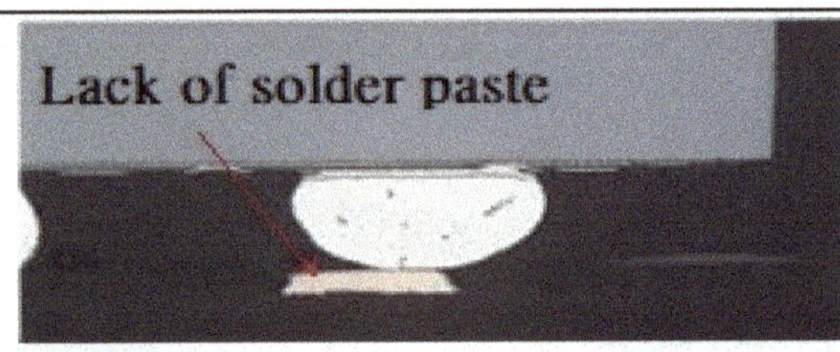
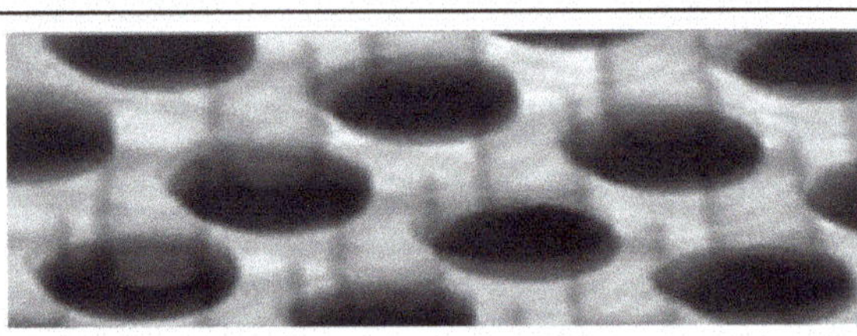	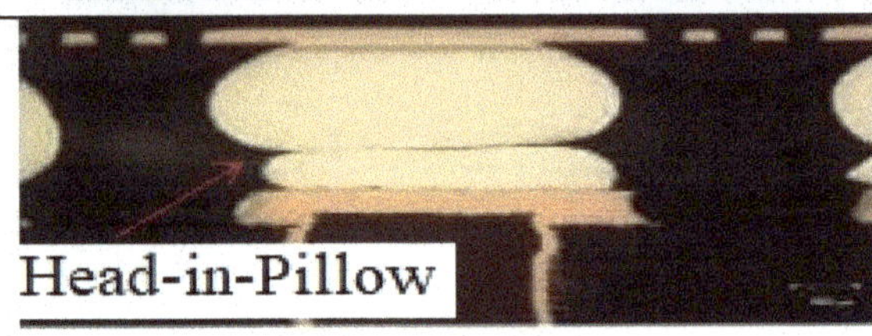
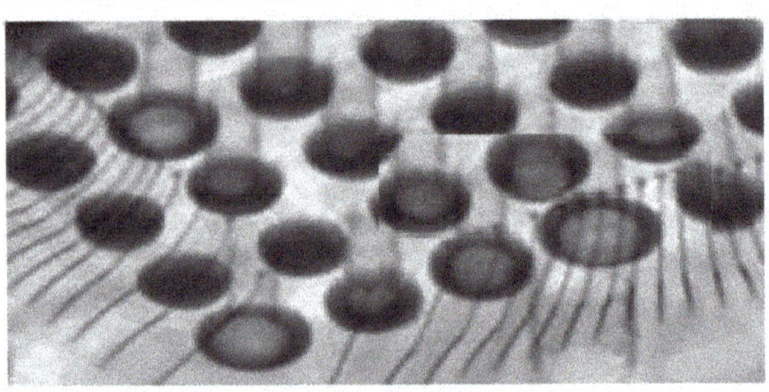	Solder paste loss 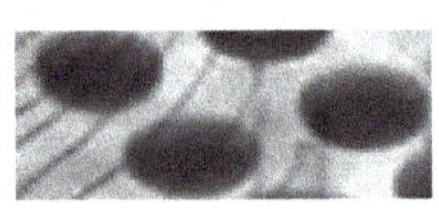 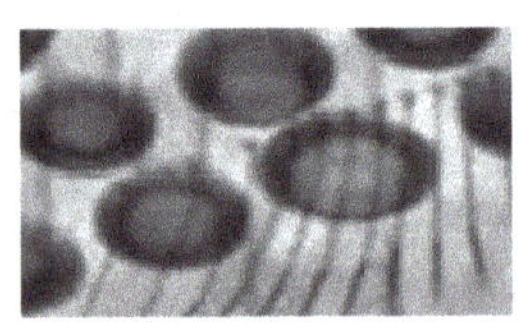
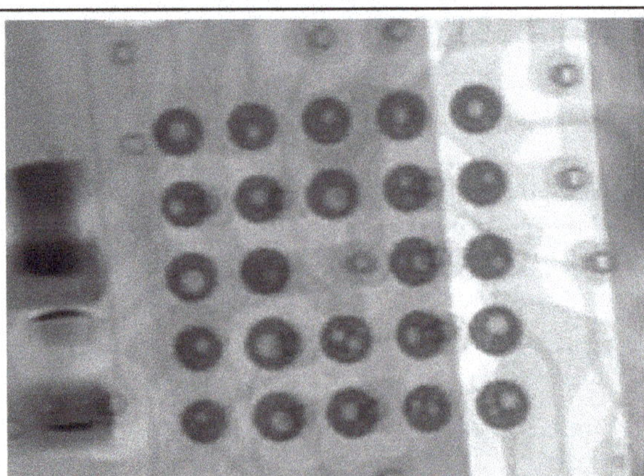	Voids 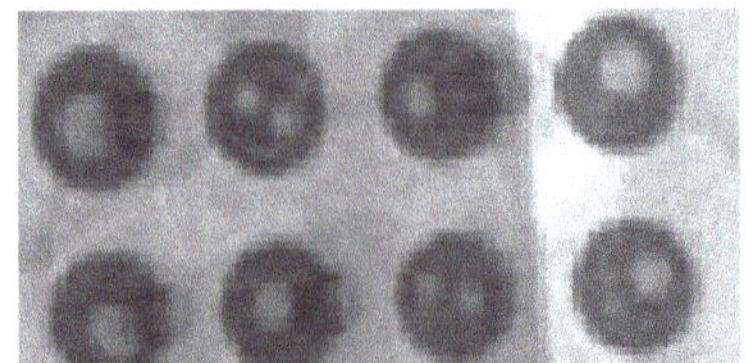

Chapter 2: Successful prevention of undesirable IC intrusion

Hollow IC

On a certain day, the defective rate of the production line exceeded 3%. After inspection, it was found that one IC was defective. There are thousands of types of ICs. It is impossible to disassemble the tray for inspection. The quality inspection unit does not have IC testing equipment. Disassembling the package will destroy the vacuum and moisture will invade the IC. The inspection can only check the number and quantity before entering the warehouse!
It just so happens that there is a problem with the quality of ICs. It seems that some ICs also need to be inspected for incoming materials.

After X-Ray comparison inspection of normal IC and failed IC, the comparison results are shown in Figures 2-1 and 2-2. Surprise! The normal IC can vaguely see the central chip and clear wire bonding. The failed IC does not even have a chip or wire bonding, only a lead frame. There is no flaw in the plastic appearance. It is a defective product that is trying to make money.

The supplier admitted that because the original factory could not deliver the goods, it temporarily bought a batch of cheap goods from Hong Kong, which did not guarantee the quality. It wanted to shirk the responsibility of burning the IC after passing through the reflow oven, but the truth was found out by X-Ray. Under the evidence, the manufacturer agreed to compensate.

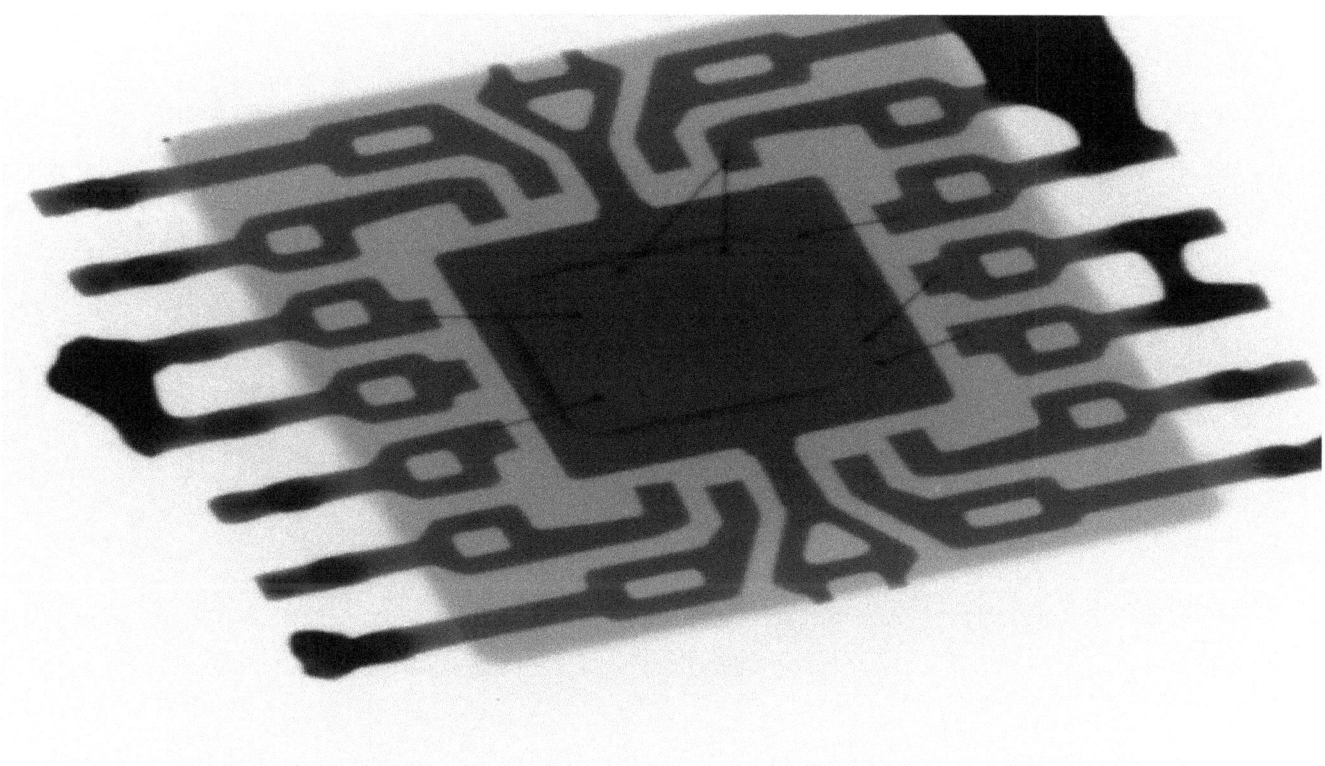

Figure 2-1. A properly functioning IC with the central silicon wafer and clear bonding wires vaguely visible

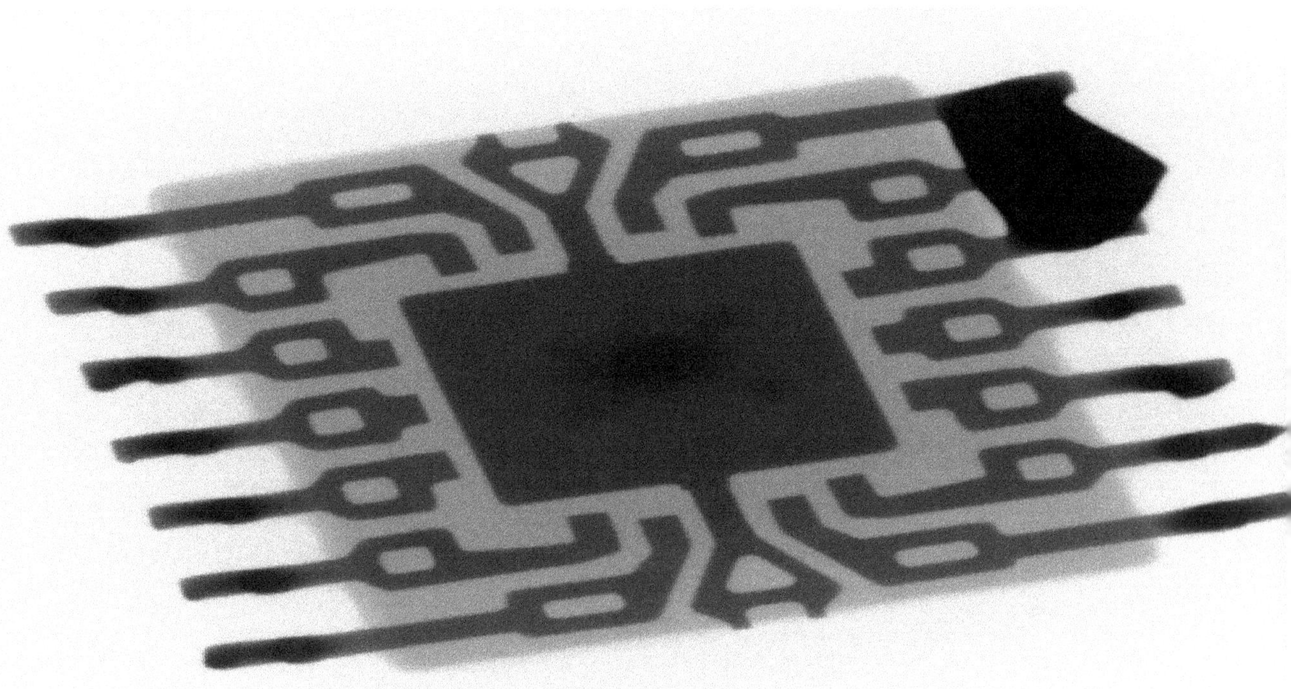

Figure 2-2. A malfunctioning IC with empty chips and wires

This case happened more than once. The left side of Figure 2-3 shows a normal electronic component, and the right side shows a failed product. Neither the chip nor the wire bonding is good. X-Ray is used again to prevent defective products from passing the test. ICs should still be purchased from original manufacturers, not from unknown sources. The production line produces in large quantities and cannot afford to make mistakes. The credibility and quality control of suppliers should be carefully reviewed.

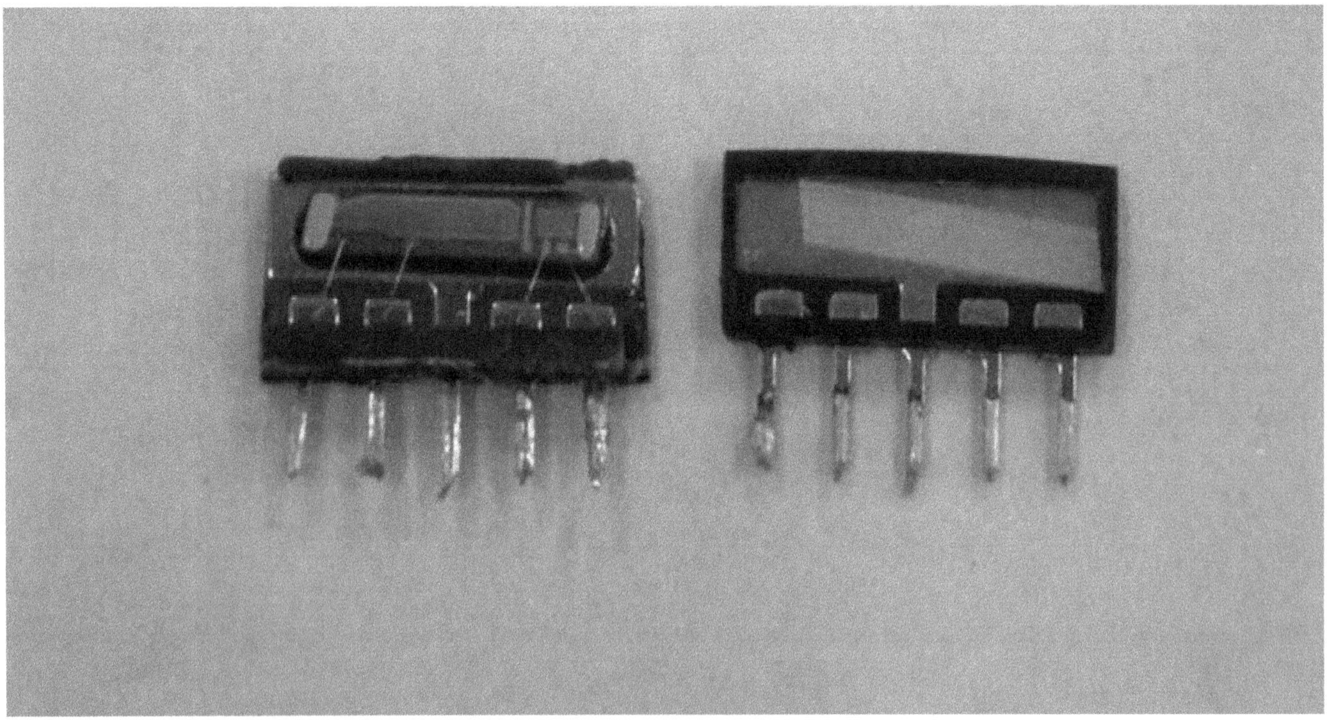

Figure 2-3. The left side is a normal product, and the right side is a malfunctioning IC with no chip and wire bonding.

BGA Solder ball residue

IC manufacturers have a low error rate and rarely conduct random inspections on incoming BGA ICs, but defects always occur. Unpacking and inspection actually reveal evidence of defects. Figure 2-4 clearly shows that there is hardened resin residue on the BGA solder ball. The entire solder ball is covered with resin and is insulated, which is a problem with the IC manufacturing process.

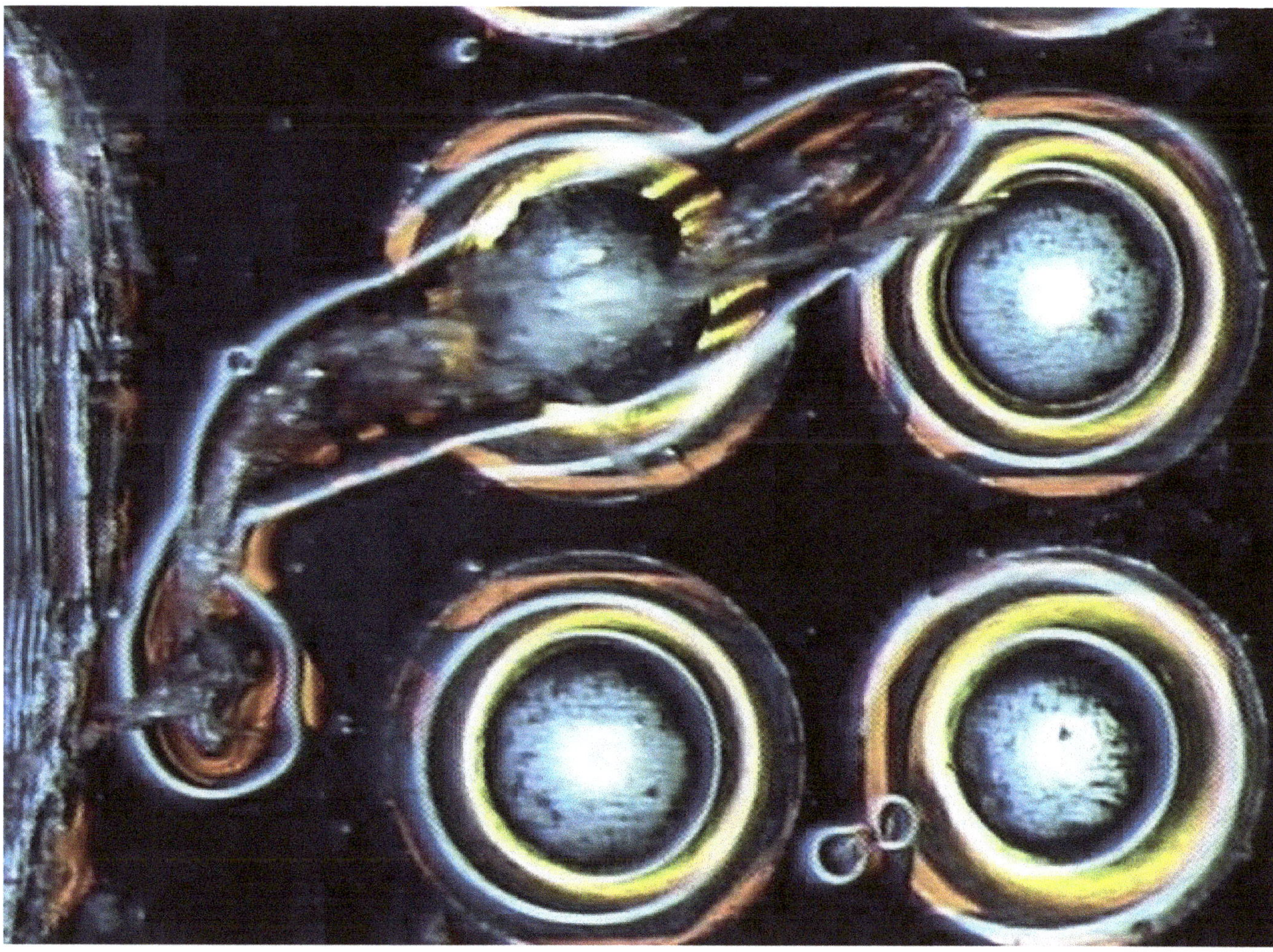

Figure 2-4. Resin residue on BGA solder balls

A game of wits with IC manufacturer

It is not easy to get IC manufacturers to admit their mistakes. After a certain IC from a large manufacturer passed through the reflow oven, the electrical function failed. The IC manufacturer pointed out that the IC failure was caused by poor processing temperature. We sent the IC to SGS for standard furnace temperature processing to prove that the IC was not heat-resistant. The result was successful.

Poor IC temperature resistance can sometimes be seen from the appearance of the IC package after temperature processing. Some unknown exposed substances, bubbles, and deformation.

Figure 2-5 is an AI simulation example.

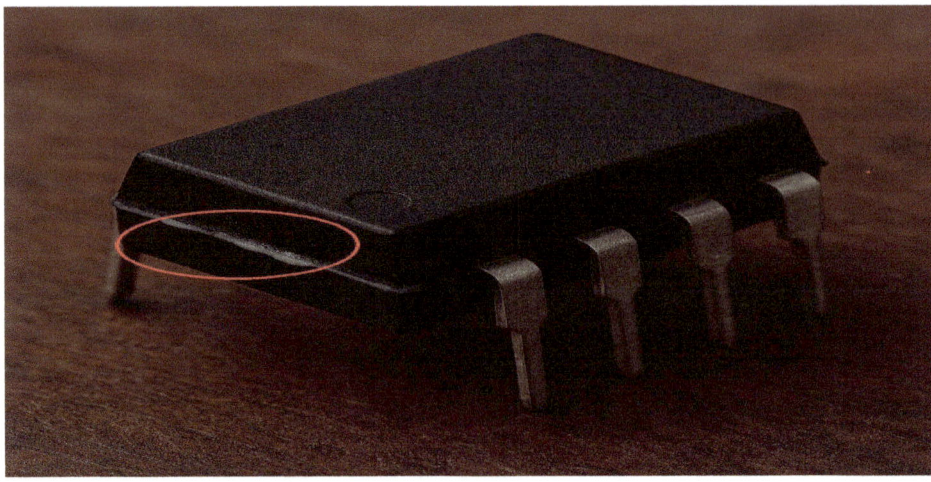

Figure 2-5. IC was not heat-resistant.

Lingshan Grand Buddha in Wuxi, China

The old Chinese proverb " clasp the Buddha's feet when danger arises " .

Chapter 3: QFN (Quad Flat No Lead)、BGA Cold welding defects

QFN Processing Technology

The bottom view of QFN IC or LCC is shown in Figure 3-1. It is an IC component with terminals hidden underneath. The cross-section image is shown in Figure 3-2.

Figure 3-1. The red circle of QFN IC is the solder pad, and the central square is the heat dissipation area and also needs to be soldered.

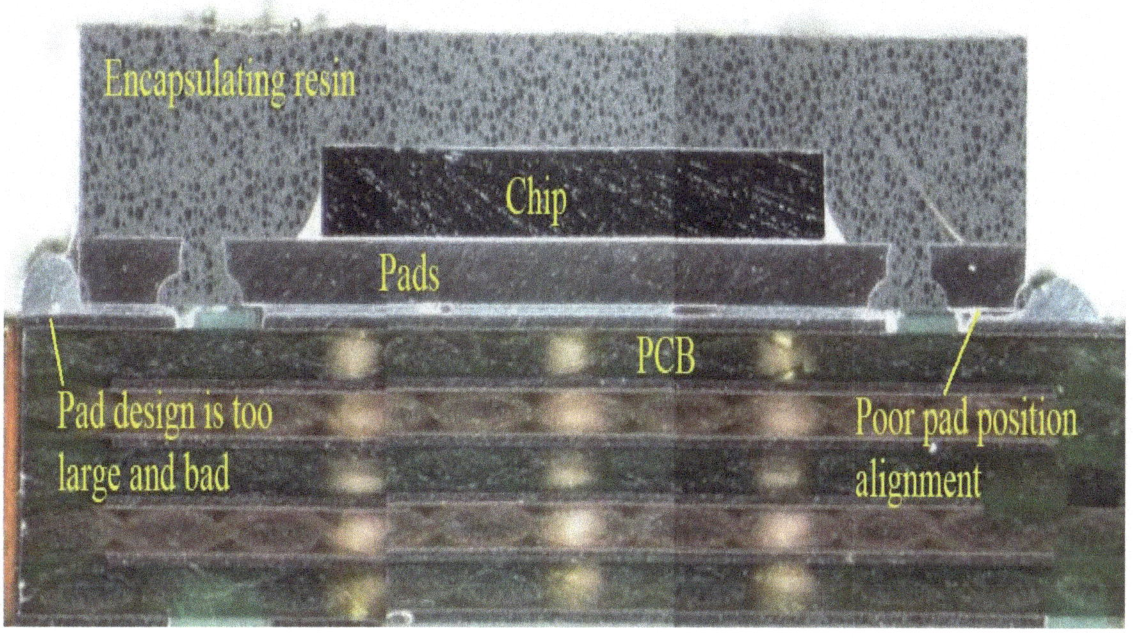

Figure 3-2. QFN cross-section image

Figure 3-2 QFN IC cross-section view, the copper foil surface of the PCB on the right does not correspond to the IC soldering pad (the soldering pad size design is poor and should be moved to the left), causing the molten tin to flow out of the IC and failing to achieve the soldering purpose, which is called poor soldering. The pad position needs to be redesigned.

The top gray area with black particles is the encapsulation resin, the central black part is the chip, the lead frame below the chip is the solder pad, and the green part is the PCB. There are two common types of QFN IC Pad foot pads. You can observe whether the metal foot pad at the bottom extends to the side of the IC. If it extends to the side, the side metal should also be tinned. The example is the type that does not extend to the side, and there is no side tinning.
During IC automated mass production, a roll of metal material is used as a lead frame to install IC chips one by one, and then cut into individual ICs after completion. Due to the cutting operation, the raw copper is exposed on the edge of the strip. After a period of time, copper becomes copper oxide, which is dark red and not easy to absorb tin. Therefore, it is unnecessary to require the side to be tinned. It is unreasonable for customers to require the side to be tinned, and there is no standard requiring tinning.

A common defect of QFN is that the PCB Pad Layout is too long. After the Reflow oven, the tin on the outside of the IC gathers into a ball shape as shown in Figure 3-3. Since the IC only has a metal pad at the bottom, this ball of tin is not helpful for solderability. The PCB design should reduce the Pad length. The external length of the PCB Pad should be 0.15-0.2 mm longer than the IC pad, and the internal length should be 0.05-0.1 mm longer than the IC pad (to absorb the error of the SMT machine). QFN Pad design is a lot of knowledge. For details, please refer to the original manufacturer's recommended dimensions.

Figure 3-3. Cross-section of QFN IC foot pad, the excess tin flows to the outside and forms a ball

SMT stencils are also very important. To quote the experience of an SMT master: "Align the center point of solder paste printing with the center point of IC pads." Because when the solder paste begins to melt, it will form a semicircular shape on the PCB due to cohesive force. If the highest point of the semicircle is aligned with the center point of the IC pad, the welding effect will be the best. The grounding plate design in the middle of the QFN IC is also very important. Remember to open some through holes for large-area grounding so that there is a place for excess molten tin to drain, to avoid a large piece of solder paste melting and pushing up the IC due to cohesive force, causing the IC side to float and poor tin absorption.

Challenges of Reflow Oven Temperature Profile

QFN often has cold soldering. The symptom is that pressing the IC sometimes makes it better. The slices in Figures 3-4 and 3-5 show a faint line between the pad and the solder paste. There is no good fusion at all, and the standard temperature is insufficient. Finally, it was found that this old QFN IC needs to reach a high temperature of 260°C and a time of 60~150 seconds, which is far more than the recommended 230-250°C and 30~60 seconds for solder paste. Reason for review failure: A common mistake made by designers is that they do not obtain the heating temperature conditions of parts such as IC, resistors, capacitors, and sockets. Usually, they only ask suppliers for size, function, and reliability test data for design, while ignoring the profile required by SMT. It is necessary to know that the heating temperature conditions of all electronic parts must be submitted to SMT production personnel for review to set an oven temperature condition that is applicable to all components. It is necessary to conduct DOE (Design of Experiment) tests, record all test conditions such as materials, furnace temperature, furnace speed, solder paste type, printer parameters, SMT stencils , etc., and test different conditions to find the best production parameters.

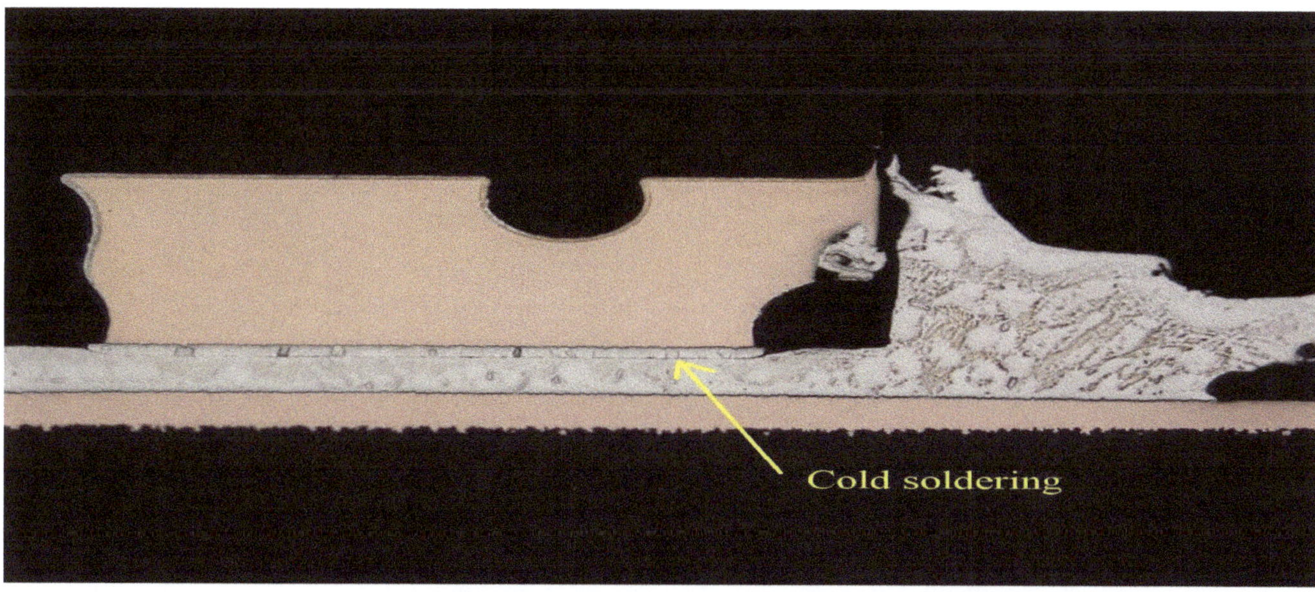

Figure 3-4. Cold soldering caused by insufficient processing temperature

Figure 3-54. Cold soldering caused by insufficient processing temperature

Chapter 4: Tactile switches, short circuit, silver migration, tin whisker defect

There are many types of tactile switches. The following figure shows the appearance and specifications.

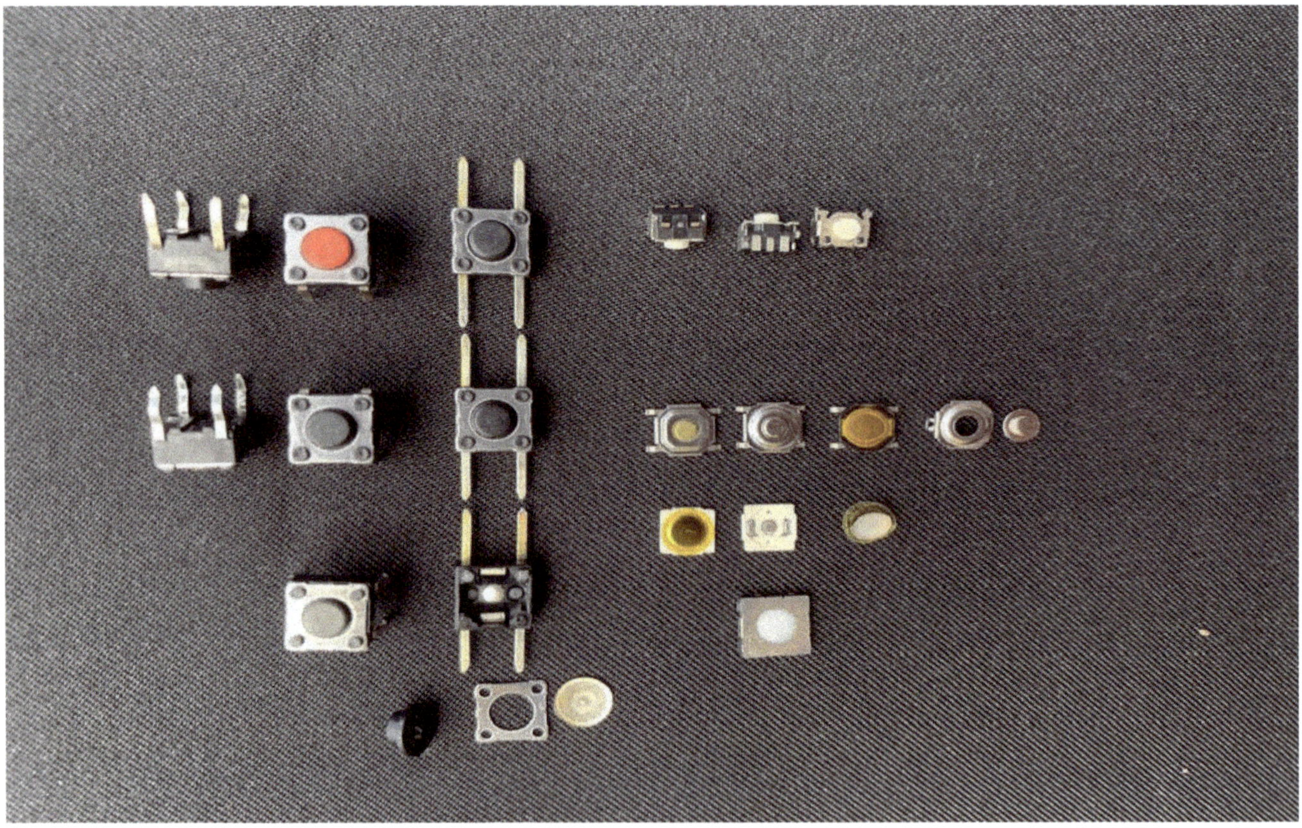

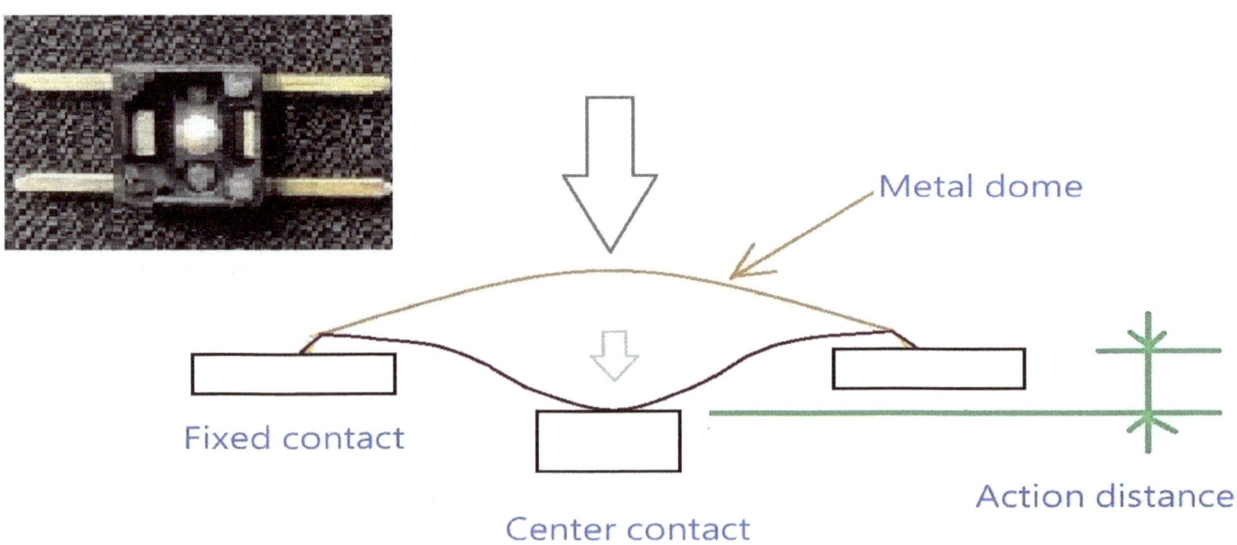

Note:

Since the automatic production machine uses a whole roll of material strips, although the TS has 4 pins, it actually only has 2 terminals. The vertical machine will cut off the upper 2 pins to expose the cut surface. Do not touch the cut 2 terminals with metal objects, which will cause a short circuit without knowing it.

【1】Setup: Force specification setting (taking 260g +-40g as an example)

No.	Item	Range	Value	Description
1、	Min Initial Force	0 – 700g：	0	Minimum initial force
2、	Max Initial Force	0 – 700g：	700	Maximum initial force
3、	Min Peak Force (F)	10 – 700g：	220	Minimum peak force
4、	Max Peak Force (F)	10 – 700g：	300	Maximum peak force
5、	Min Click Force (C)	1 – 700g：	60	Minimum click force
6、	Max Click Force (C)	1 – 700g：	260	Maximum click force
7、	Max On Force	1 – 700g：	700	Maximum value of on-state force
8、	End Test Force	100 – 700g：	300	Test end strength
9、	Min Peak POS (SP)	1 – 700（0.01mm）：	5	Minimum force position
10、	Max Peak POS (SP)	1 – 700（0.01mm）：	35	Maximum force position
11、	Min Stroke (ST)	99 – 999（0.01mm）：	15	Minimum stroke
12、	Max Stroke (ST)	99 – 999（0.01mm）：	35	Maximum stroke
13、	Min ON timing (ON)	99 – 999（0.01mm）：	-1	Minimum switch ON point
14、	Max ON timing (ON)	99 – 999（0.01mm）：	3	Maximum switch ON point
15、	Min Click % (C%)	1 – 50（%）：	30	CLICK percentage lower limit
16、	Max Click % (C%)	10 – 90（%）：	80	CLICK percentage upper limit
17、	Min Restore Force (R)	10 – 600g：	60	Minimum restoring force
18、	ON Force > Peak	-99 – 999g：	0	ON Force Limit Value
19、	Debug Code	0 – 9999：	1234	Operation password
20、	Load Cell distance	offset ±3：	0	distance compensation
90、	LOT Number :			Enter the production lot name
99、	Save	FILENAME :		Save files
00、	Quit or （Return）	【Select】：		Quit or （Return）

The force curve of the tactile switch is shown in the figure below. The initial pressure of the tactile switch is zero

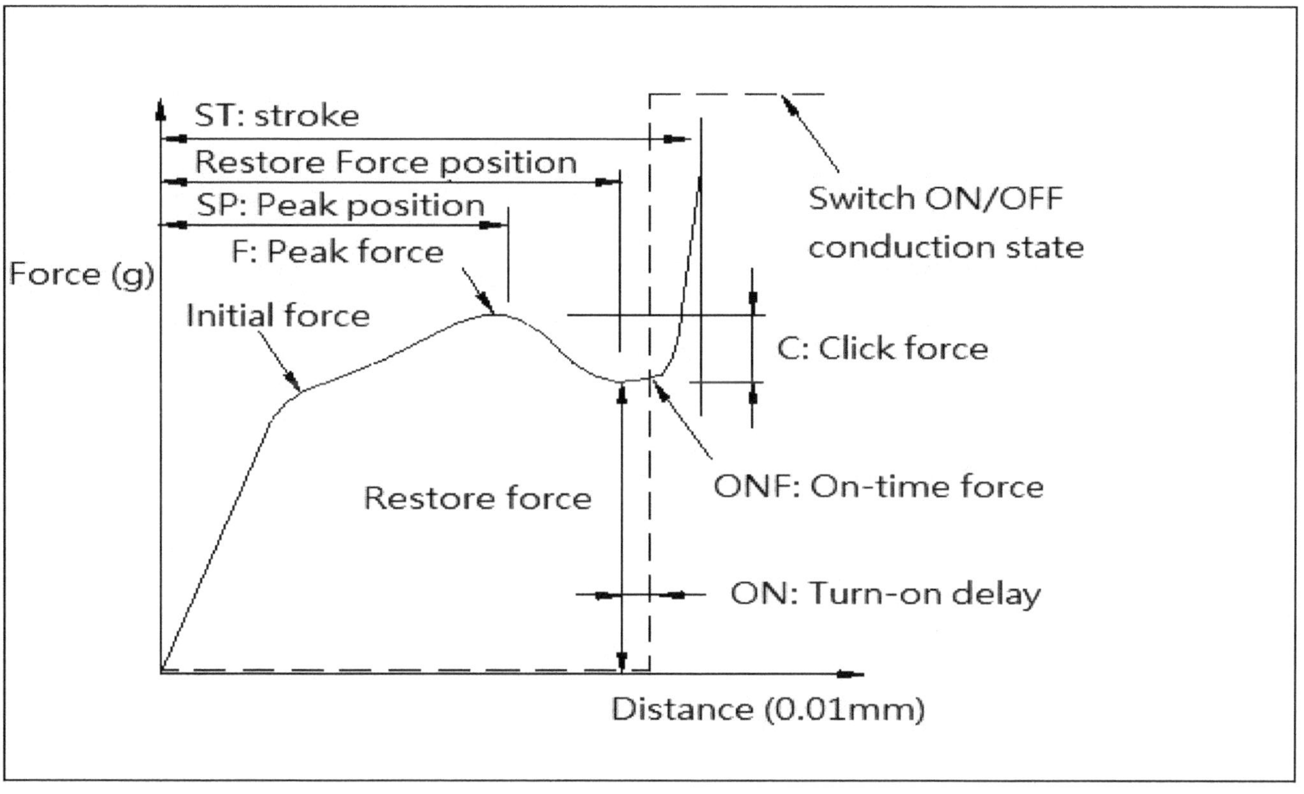

Silver Migration

Market response: The adjustment menu keeps appearing on the monitor screen, which means that the switch is always on. The sample was measured with a Digital Multimeter (DMM) to confirm that the tactile switch is indeed on without being pressed. After disassembling and checking, it was found that a gradient metal extended from the metal fixed contact inside the tactile switch as shown in Figure 4-1. The sample was sent to a laboratory for analysis using an EDX energy dispersive spectrometer. Figure 4-1 shows the three sampling points inside the tactile switch for EDX analysis.

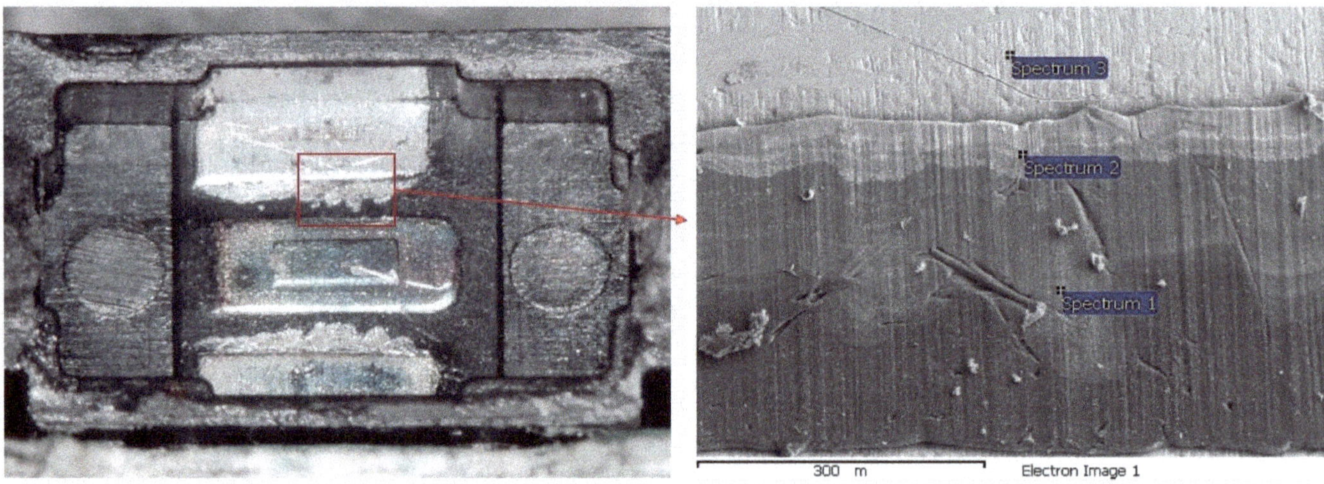

Figure 4-1. Silver diffusion migration failure

EDX Energy dispersive spectrometr [Classification: Destructive analysis]

Figure 4-2 is a photo of the appearance of the EDX equipment. Its principle is to use a high-energy electron beam as an emission excitation source, project and focus the electron beam on the substance to be tested, and the high-energy electron beam excites the test substance to produce X-rays. The energy of the excited X-rays is used to analyze its elemental composition. EDX analysis method is often used for inorganic compound analysis (inorganic compounds generally refer to compounds of elements other than carbon).

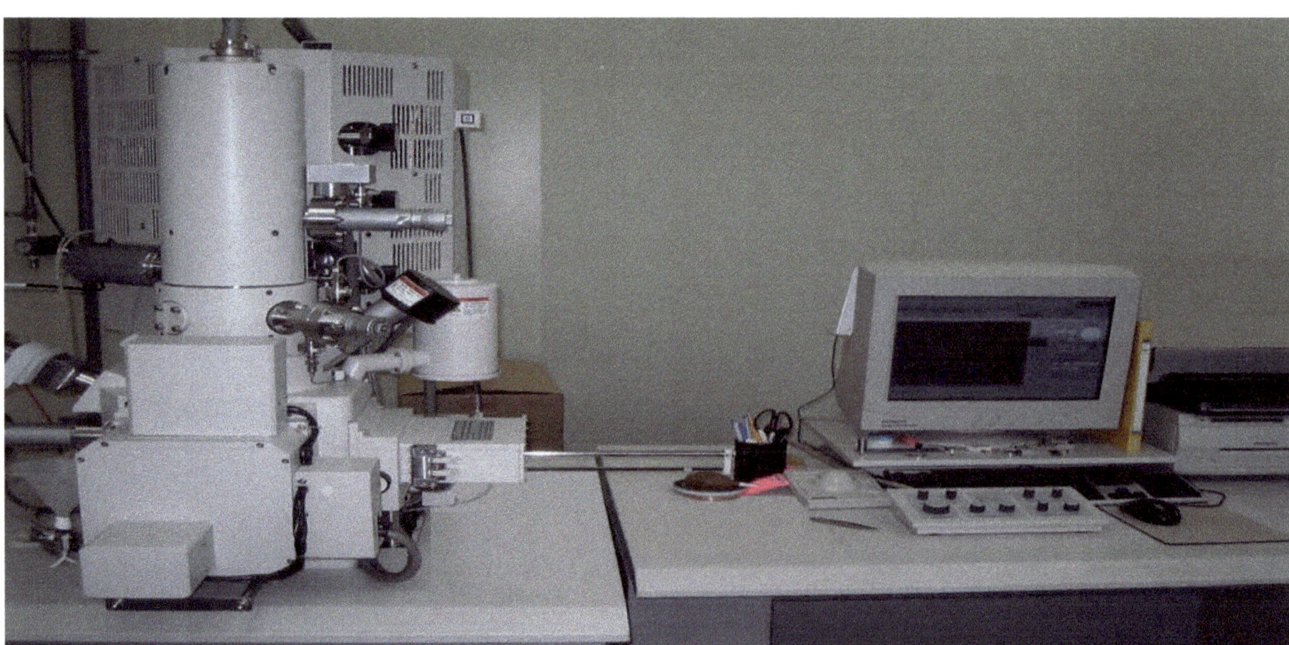

Figure 4-2. EDX energy dispersive spectrometer

The EDX analysis results are shown in Figure 4-3. The third point has the highest silver content (element symbol: Ag) of 85.64%. This sampling point is on the metal terminal. The metal terminal is originally copper (Cu) with nickel (Ni) as the base. The surface is treated with silver plating for good conductivity. It is normal that the silver content of the surface layer is the highest. The first and second points are on the plastic. The second point has a silver content of 51.03%, and the first point has a silver content of 45.21%. The silver content gradually decreases, which is consistent with the concentration distribution of the migration phenomenon.

Reminder: EDX requires cutting a small piece of the object for analysis and electroplating a layer of platinum (platinum Pt) when used for non-metallic conductor analysis, which will destroy the original sample and is a destructive analysis.

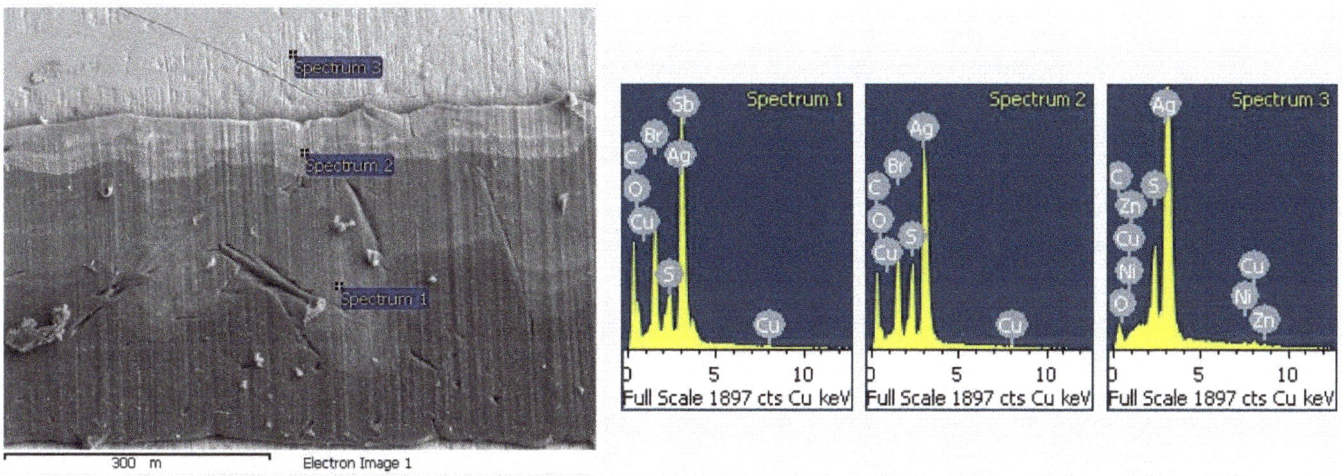

Spectrum	C	O	S	Ni	Cu	Zn	Br	Ag	Sb	Total
Spectrum 1	18.93	12.5	2.89	-	1.14	-	12.7	45.21	6.64	100
Spectrum 2	20.55	8.55	6.07	-	1.87	-	11.93	51.03	-	100
Spectrum 3	1.25	1.59	4.89	0.97	3.69	1.96	-	85.64	-	100

" - " means below the detection limit *All results in weight%*

Figure 4-3. Silver diffusion migration analysis results

Figure 4-4 shows another type of switch silver migration case. The phenomenon is electrochemical migration (ECM). The phenomenon is the growth of branch-like structures, which causes the switch to short-circuit. Microscopic observation and short-circuit measurement with a multimeter can reveal the problem.

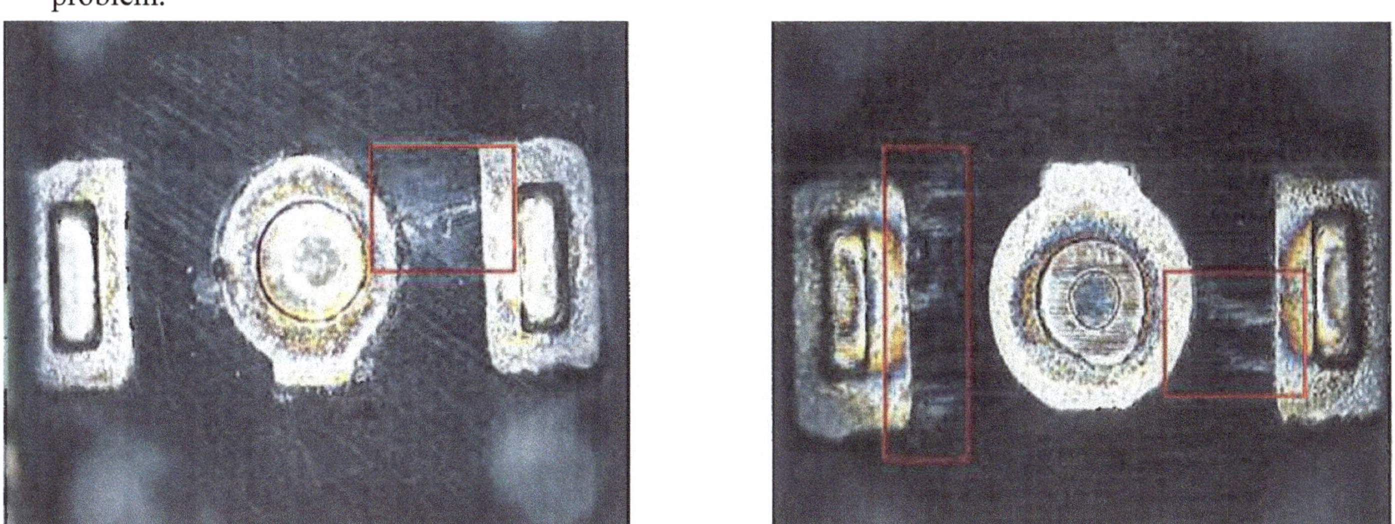

Figure 4-4. Silver migration ECM defect

Aanalysis case conducted by Japan showed that the problem was silver migration short circuit.

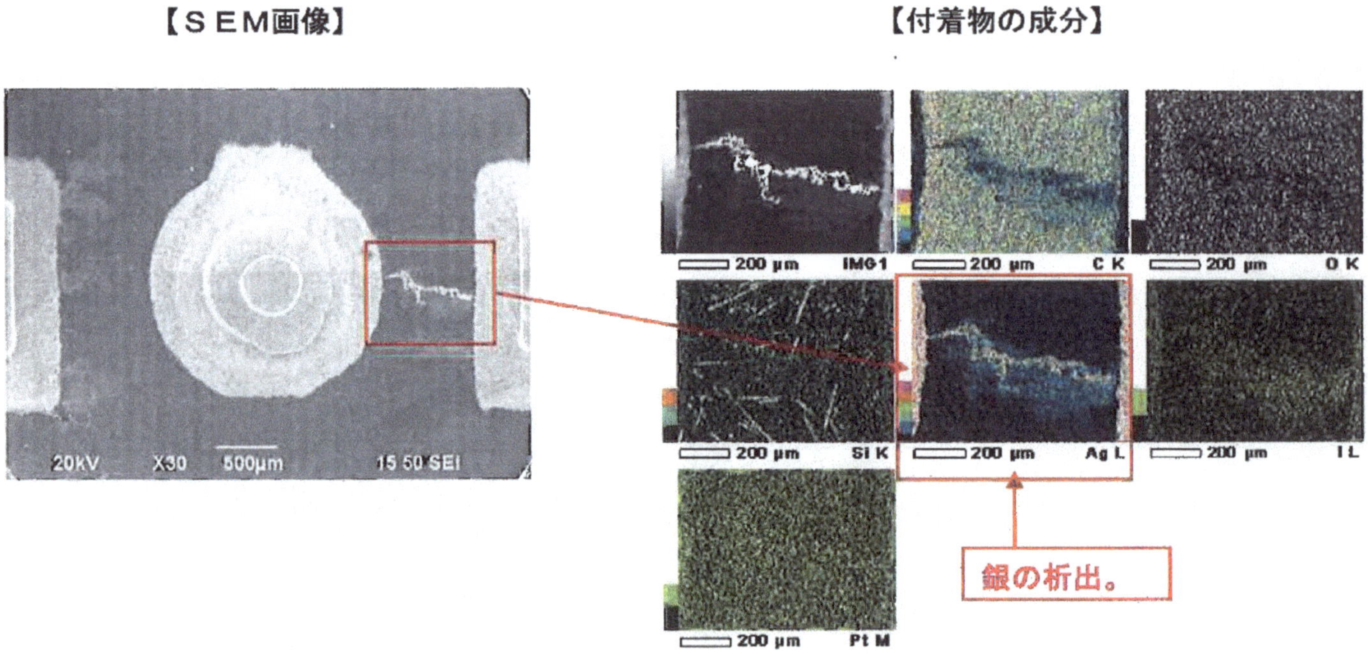

Figure 4-5. Silver Migration (ECM) Fault Analysis Report

Reviewing the causes of electrochemical migration (ECM), during the long-term aging process in a high temperature and high humidity environment between two adjacent silver conductors, the silver metal causes the migration of silver ions due to the DC potential difference, resulting in insulation degradation and even short circuit and leakage. The main conditions for occurrence are the DC potential difference plus the high temperature and high humidity environment, especially moisture.

The customer proposed to strengthen waterproofing, add an insulating layer, moisture-proof, clean and remove acidic substances, etc., but we thought about other solutions. The general composition of metal terminals is a copper base material plus a nickel plating layer, and finally silver plating. Silver plating has excellent conductivity and low contact impedance, and is only used in high-end products.

If a thick nickel plating layer is added to the copper terminal, the silver migration effect can also be suppressed. Changing the waterproof structure requires moving the mold structure, which is not a good method in terms of cost and time. Finally, the silver plating was changed to a cheaper tin plating treatment to reduce costs.

Switch stuck

The metal dome was placed in a position deviation during assembly, and one side was stuck on the plastic side, causing poor switch operation. Figure 4-6 shows the problem point with X-Ray perspective. The key points for improvement are the positioning accuracy adjustment of the vacuum suction nozzle of the metal dome , the proper control of the vacuum force during placement to avoid blowing over the metal dome, cleaning the nozzle to avoid sticking, etc.

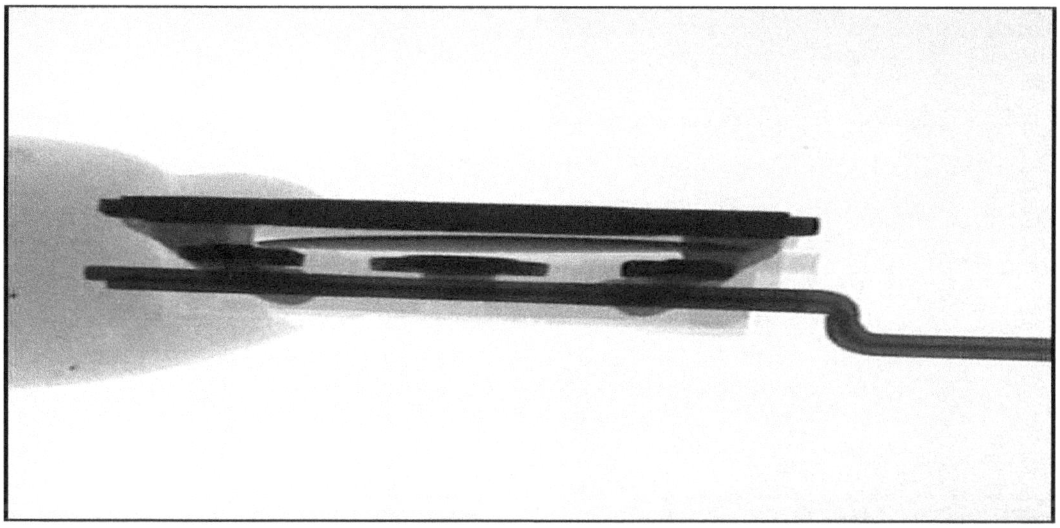

Figure 4-6. Tactile switch stuck phenomenon

Metal shavings, Solder balls,Splatter

Figure 4-7. The cause of the failure is very obvious, a metal wire crosses the contact. In the automated assembly process, many stations have metal cutting operations, which inevitably produce metal shavings. Metal shavings fall into the circuit and cause a short circuit.

The treatment measures are:

1. Check the cutting tools. When the tools are ware, they will tear and tear to produce metal shavings. Set a life management, such as disassembling and checking the tools or re-grinding the tools one million times.
2. Add vacuum cleaning, blowing or brushing stations. If you are in a clean room, it is not recommended to use dust blowing to avoid blowing everywhere and causing pollution.
3. Increase the number of daily cleaning times for the machine and do a good job of 6S management.

Figure 4-7. Metal wire residue causing short circui

Solder balls

Figure 4-8 shows a solder ball falling between two terminals, causing a short circuit. Soldering solder balls involves adjusting preheating temperature to reduce solder explosion, furnace temperature, heating ramp rate, pad design, stencil aperture, solder paste quality, flux type, pad shape, printing accuracy and thickness, placement pressure, and moisture absorption on unbaked boards.

There are many countermeasures to consider, and solder balls can also be thrown out when soldering components with a soldering iron, which also requires attention.

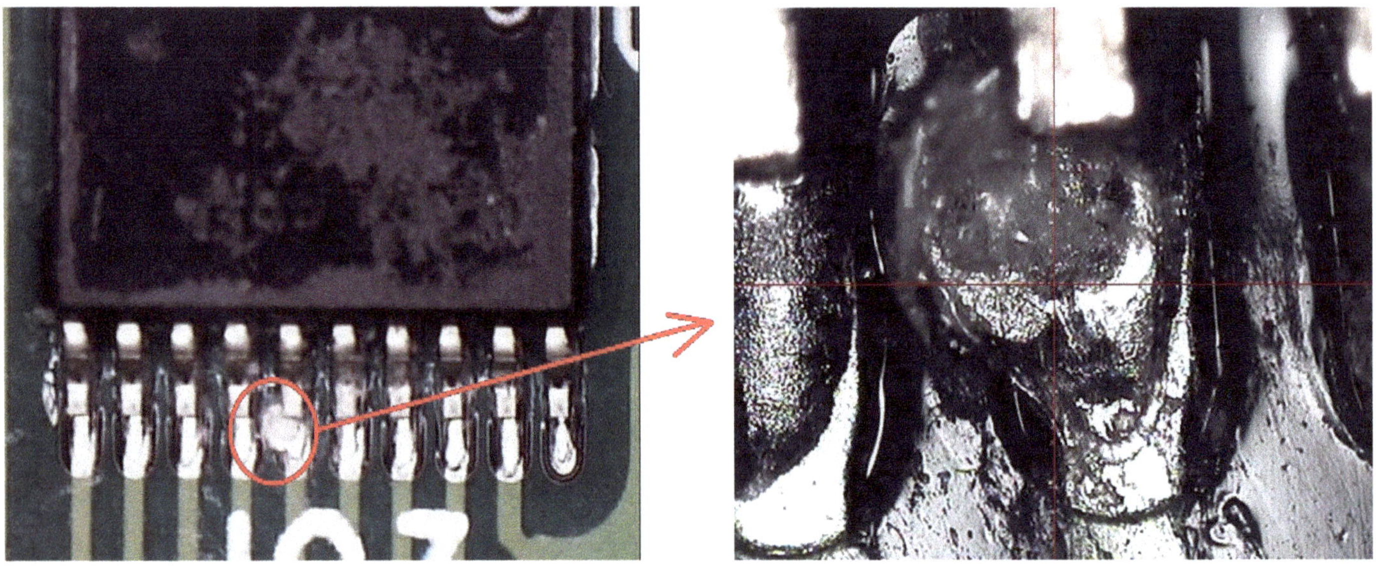

Figure 4-8. Short circuit caused by solder beads

Tin whiskers and burrs

Tin whiskers and burrs can also cause short circuits. The electroplated tin on the component surface is subjected to stress during solder solidification, as well as mechanical stresses such as plugging and unplugging, and thermal expansion and contraction from thermal shock. These stresses can easily generate burrs of several hundred micrometers (300-700 micrometers). Therefore, tin-plated products require tin whisker testing and evaluation.

Galvanized materials also require careful attention to ensure the proper material, plating, and heat treatment to prevent the formation of tin whiskers and burrs.

Tin whisker short circuits are difficult to occur immediately in tin-plated products. Fortunately, we did not encounter such adverse conditions, but the customer required a test certificate. The verification fee was about US$3,3000. The verification plan was as follows: The temperature and humidity chamberwas set at 85°C, humidity 85% RH, 1000 hours, and a batch of products were made under the conditions of power on and power off. After completion, electron microscope SEM was used for photo inspection. All tests are expensive! The test results passed.

Exploring the causes of tin whiskers:

1. Interdiffusion between tin and copper forms a metallic compound, causing a rapid increase in compressive stress within the tin layer. This causes tin atoms to squeeze and diffuse along crystal boundaries, forming tin whiskers.
2. Residual stress in the coating after electroplating leads to the growth of tin whiskers.

Solution:

1. Electroplating pure tin to matte tin changes the crystal structure and reduces stress. Alternatively, use a tin paste containing indium, bismuth, etc.
2. Bake at approximately 150°C and anneal for 2 hours.
3. Add a small amount of organic metal additives in the tinning process to limit the formation of tin-copper metal compounds.
4. Add a barrier layer such as a nickel layer between tin and copper. Usually, the metal terminal is composed of copper + nickel plating + tin plating (surface) from the inner layer.

Appreciation for a good article: Electrochemical ECM migration short circuit phenomenon. (viewed using Ssfari) Source:surfacemountprocess.com
https://www.youtube.com/shorts/nD15N453Uz4?feature=share

A photo of Jiangnan's landscape

Chapter 5: Tactile sw sulfide, Flux, salination, carbon deposition, verdigris

Sulfuration

A customer reported that their tactile switch sometimes switched on and sometimes didn't, a phenomenon known as unstable conduction. A micro-ohmmeter was used to confirm that the contact resistance exceeded the specified 100 mΩ. A photo of the meatl dome inside the switch is shown in Figure 5-1. After a period of time, such as three months or six months, the silver plating on the metal dome undergoes a sulfurization reaction.

This sulfurization causes the silver sulfide in the silver-white silver plating layer on the metal dome to discolor black. The darker the color, the more severe the sulfurization. The gradual thickening of the silver sulfide layer affects the switch's electrical conductivity. Silver sulfide causes the switch's contact resistance to exceed 100 mΩ, resulting in insensitivity.

EDX analysis can directly measure sulfur (S). Sources of sulfur in the environment include acid rain from coal burning, oil refining, automobile exhaust, clothing bleach, bleached wrapping paper, and sulfur treatment during tire rubber processing. (Sulfur is added to rubber during the rubber manufacturing process to adjust its elasticity. Rubber bands, for example, contain sulfur, which can also cause silver discoloration.)

The solution to the sulfidation phenomenon is to coat the silver-plated surface with a layer of anti-sulfur material. As for the anti-sulfur formula and concentration, each factory has its own technical secrets. Japanese technology is better and relatively expensive. To test the anti-sulfur effect, you can use a 2% K2S test agent and soak for 10 seconds to see the effect.

Different degrees of brown discoloration. Figure 5-2 shows the effect of different concentrations of coating on anti-sulfurization. The top test piece is completely uncoated with anti-sulfur material and almost turns black. The best effect is 100% coating.

Another countermeasure is to replace the electroplating material, replacing silver plating with gold plating, so there is no sulfidation problem.

After treatment, the anti-sulfur treatment can withstand several months of use. Anti-sulfurization treatment will increase the cost. Whether to use it depends on the price of the product. High-end products such as audio and instruments are better, while toys compete with low prices, such as changing silver plating to tin plating, which is less expensive.

Stamping processing will also lead to the destruction of the anti-sulfur effect, so the greater the metal bending, the greater the damage to the anti-sulfur effect, so the discoloration around is more serious than the center, as shown in Figure 5-1

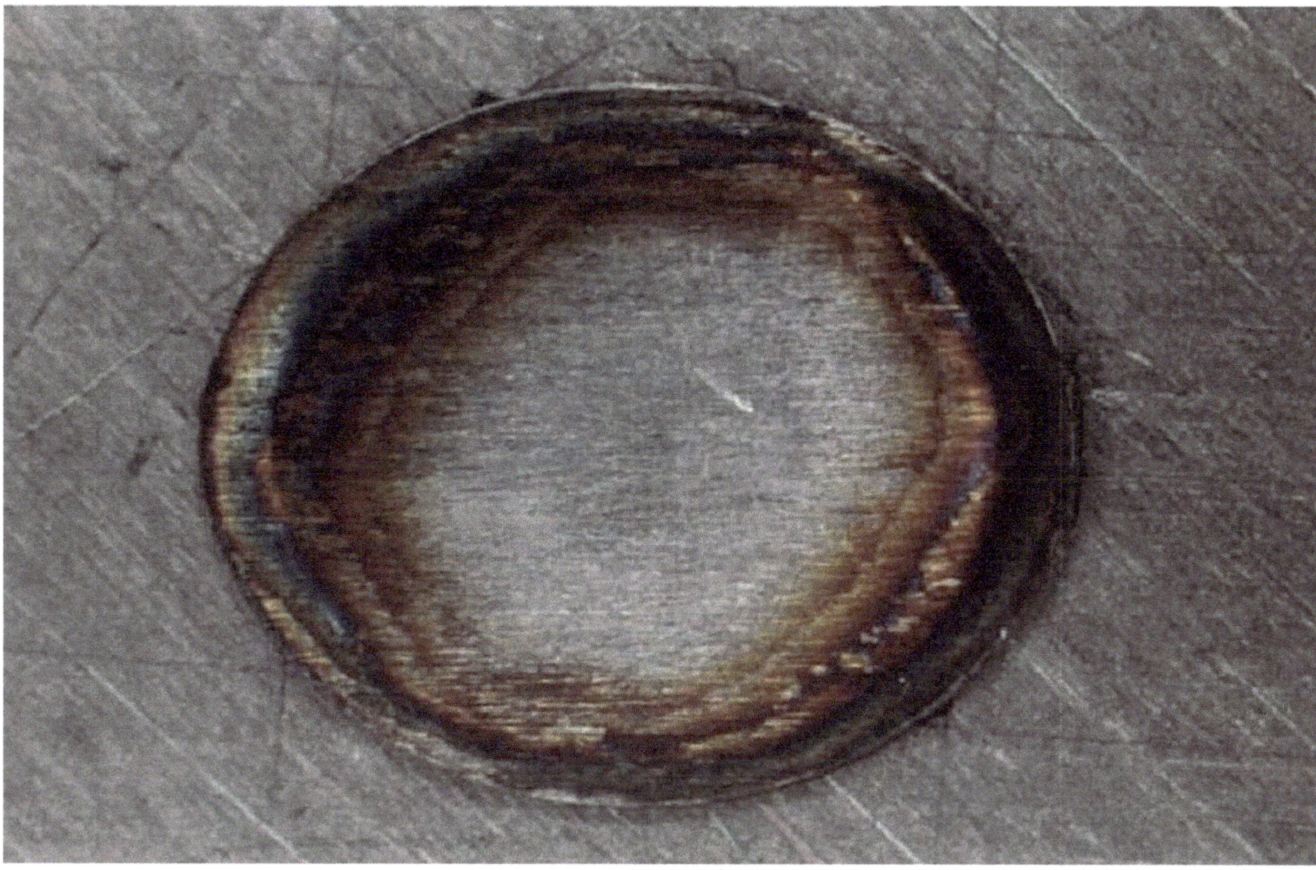

Figure 5-1. Sulfurization of the silver-plated metal dome inside the tactile switch

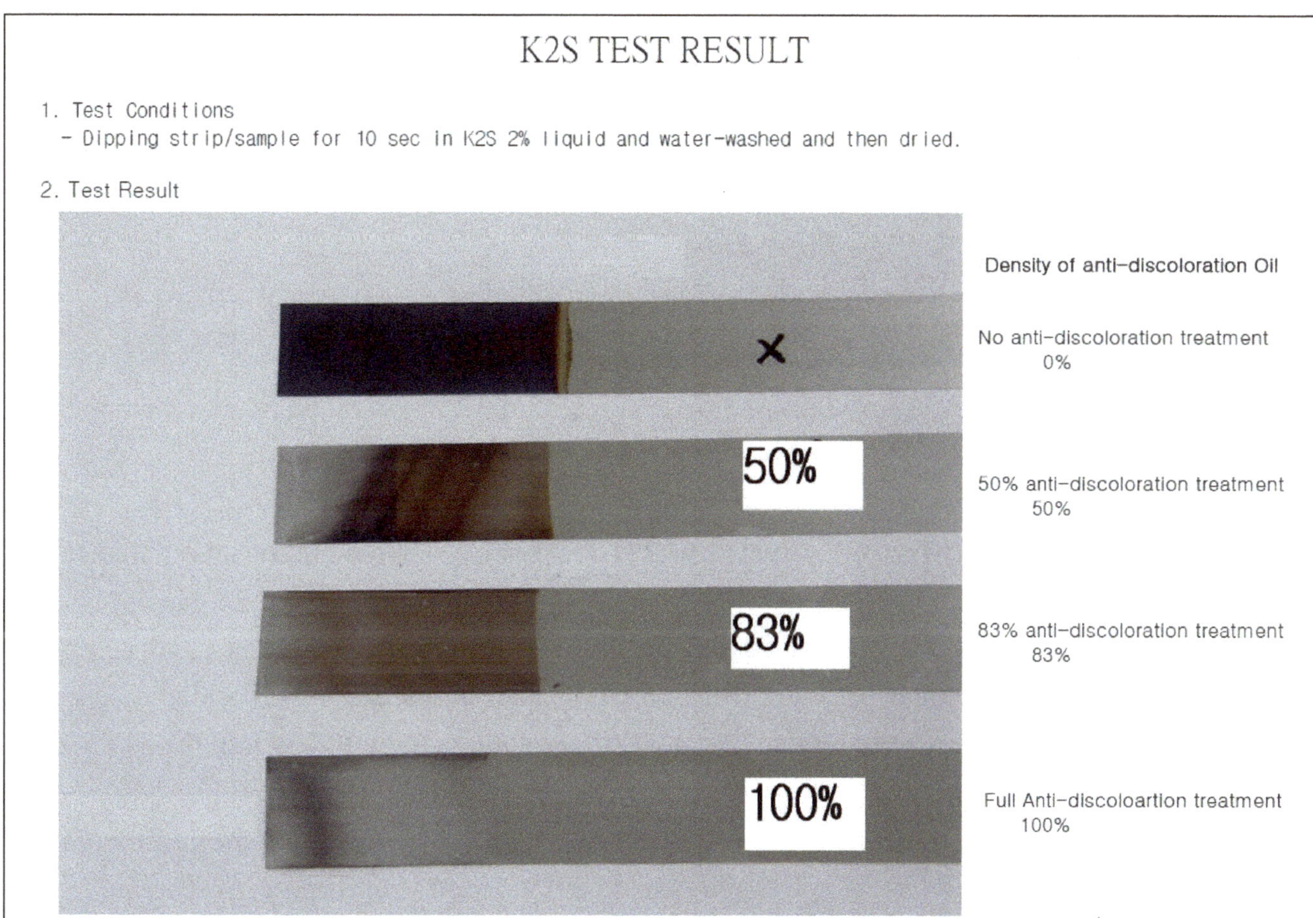

Figure 5-2. K2S test evaluation results after anti-sulfur treatment

Flux intrusion

The SMT reflow oven and DIP oven are used in the customer's processing. The rosin flux added to the solder paste volatilizes into gas, which can easily invade the inside of the switch. Unclean or poor quality Flux forms salt crystals after drying, and its non-conductive insulation properties will cause the switch to fail. Ordinary switches have no airtightness or waterproof effects, and it is difficult to block Flux gas. For example, for connector terminal products, Flux adhesion often causes poor contact events.

Flux can be transparent and colorless, but can also be light green (containing chlorine) or light yellow. Figure 5-3 shows transparent and colorless fluid on both terminals. Because the switch has a circular, movable metal dome inside, the flux is distributed in an arc around the metal dome. The transparent grease in the lower half of the image, but no fluid in the center, indicates that the fluid entered from outside. Careful inspection will reveal the entry path. This defect is the customer's fault.

Figure 5-3. Flux intrusion from the outside, with the transparent liquid distributed in a semicircular arc.

Fourier Transform Infrared Spectrometer (FTIR): [Non-destructive analysis]

FTIR is used to confirm that the intruding material is Flux. FTIR infrared spectrometers are an excellent tool for analyzing foreign matter. For example, if foreign matter intrudes into the backlight panel, causing white or black spots on the screen, this is due to foreign matter intruding into the panel.

FTIR identifies compounds through the infrared absorption spectrum generated by the transfer of kinetic energy caused by molecules absorbing infrared radiation. It utilizes the absorption of specific wavelengths of infrared light by functional groups within the compound molecules to observe the molecular structure. When infrared light is irradiated on a sample, the resulting photocurrent is transformed through Fourier transform calculations to form the sample's characteristics. FTIR's rapid qualitative analysis of molecular structure allows the determination of the chemical structure of the sample within tens of seconds, enabling swift and effective treatment of foreign matter.

FTIR requires little to no sample preparation. As long as the analyte is present at a sufficient concentration and there is minimal background interference, reliable infrared spectra can be directly measured, regardless of whether the sample is solid, liquid, or gaseous. Tip: Create an FTIR database of both environmental background contaminants and product materials. Unidentified contaminants can be compared to this database to quickly identify the source of contamination.

Unlike EDX analysis, FTIR analysis is commonly used for analyzing organic compounds (organic compounds are a general term for carbon-containing compounds, hydrocarbons, and their derivatives). Compared to EDX, it also analyzes chemical bonds between atoms and the composition of compounds. It can easily identify rosin and resin in flux. Figure 5-4 shows the FTIR analysis report for foreign matter on switch contacts. The top red line represents the defective sample. Comparison results with the database show that the first item, rosin, has a 95.28% similarity. Resin also appears in the following items, making it straightforward to conclude that the foreign matter is flux.

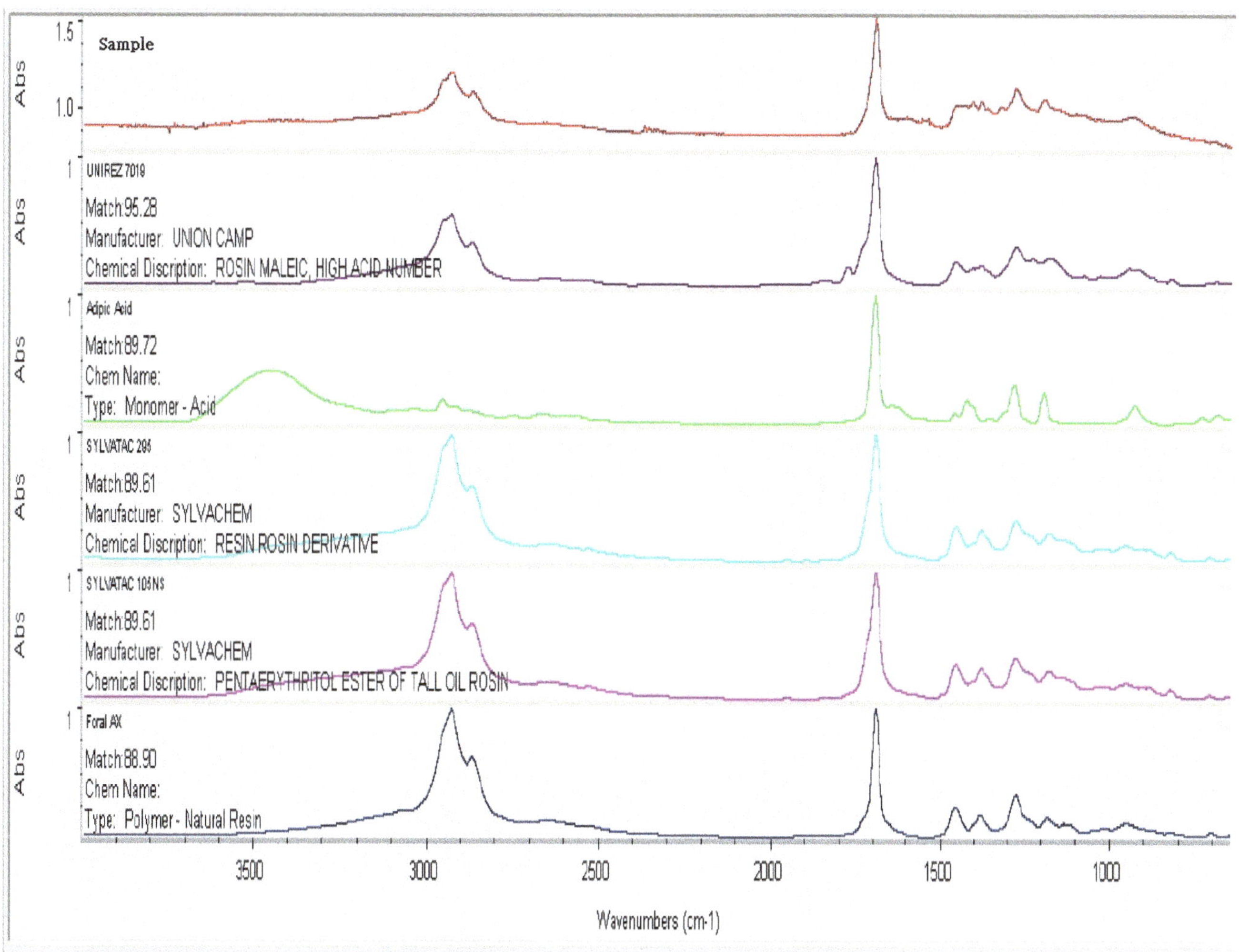

Figure 5-4. FTIR analysis report of foreign matter on switch contacts

A customer encountered a manufacturing process issue and suggested a waterproof switch as a solution. However, changing the material was a major undertaking and required the final buyer's approval. Most opted for process improvements. The suggested improvements are as follows:

● Wave soldering process:

When flux is sprayed onto the bottom of a substrate and passed through a high-temperature soldering furnace, the volatilized flux flows from the substrate's bottom to the sides in a vortex-like flow, impacting components along the board's edges. If a carrier is used for production, the flux must bypass the carrier's edges and travel a distance before reaching components on the front. During this safe distance, most of the flux is already drawn away by the exhaust or adheres to the carrier's edges.

Figure 5-5 shows an example of carrier flux prevention. Connectors, sockets, switches, and gold fingers all need to be protected from flux penetrating into components and causing poor contact. As shown on the right side of Figure 5-5, it's best to add a cover to minimize the path for flux to reach the components on the substrate.

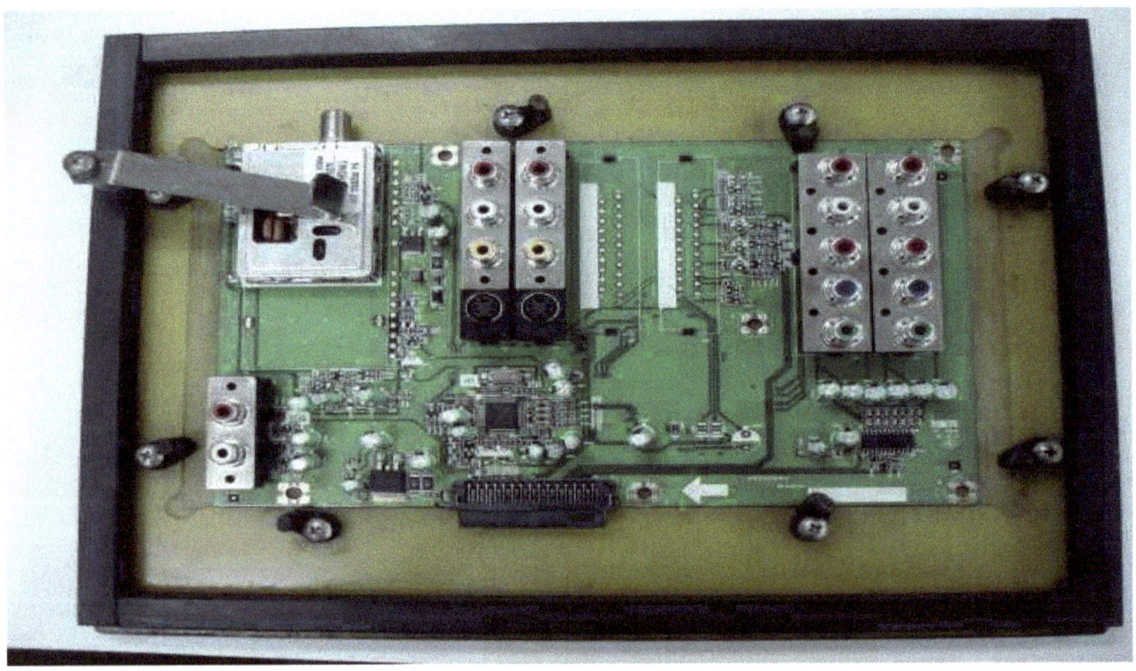

Figure 5-5. Adding a fixture to prevent Flux from entering electronic components

The exhaust speed was increased (1.0 m/s → 1.5 m/s or higher), the amount of flux sprayed was reduced (from foaming method to spray method), the furnace was cleaned regularly to remove residual resin, the preheat temperature was increased, the chain speed was reduced, the PCB drilling size was reduced to reduce the flux rising path, the PCB positioning holes/through holes were modified and shifted to prevent flux from spraying in through the through holes, the type of solder paste was changed (no resin residue after soldering, low solid content), and the selection was reviewed with the solder paste supplier...etc.

Rosin can also enter the interior of the parts through the terminals due to capillary action. Applying an anti-wicking agent is also a viable method.

- Reflow process:

Improvements included increasing exhaust volume, cleaning the furnace regularly, increasing preheating time, raising temperature, reviewing with solder paste suppliers, changing solder paste types (no resin residue after soldering), making the SMT stencil opening smaller, and reducing solder paste volume.

- Manual soldering operation:

Review and replace any solder wire with minimal rosin residue, using a protective jig to cover it. Finally, review the PCBA cleaning process. Avoid cleaning components like switches and connectors. Especially note: Flux + IPA (isopropyl alcohol) can produce white crystalline phosphate. This has occurred in some cases where salification occurred a week later, resulting in insulation.

Confirm that the flux does not chemically react with the cleaning agent. This can be discussed with the solder paste supplier. Always check the cleaning agent bottle on your work surface for contamination and discoloration. Replace it regularly, as this is a common area of concern.

Plastic debris foreign matter intrusion

Foreign matter intrusion into products is a common customer complaint in the industry. Factories like backlight and LCD factories maintain extremely high cleanliness standards. Even wearing anti-static cleanroom clothing, covering your entire body with only your eyes exposed, can still be difficult to eliminate. Even after smoking, the smoke particles in your breath remain a source of contamination for several minutes, so smokers are prohibited from entering high-grade cleanrooms for 30 minutes.

Remember to create an FTIR database of foreign matter in the workplace (plastics, cloth, paper, dust, glue, etc.). Comparing contaminants with FTIR analysis can identify the source of contamination and enable corrective measures. Figures 5-6 show photos of foreign matter inside a switch. Microscope analysis confirmed it was plastic shavings, but the client requested scientific evidence, so FTIR analysis was performed.

Figures 5-7 The foreign matter was analyzed by FTIR and compared with the database, and the closest similarity was 69.18% for various Nylon (engineering plastics). the material used for plastic housings. When the plastic is sliced very thinly, its color appears translucent gray.

The cause in this case was misalignment during the placement of the central metal dome component. The offset circular metal dome scraped out plastic shavings, as shown in the image.

Figures 5-6. Plastic debris

	Index	Match	Compound Name	Library Name
1	15	69.18	Nylon 6	Sprouse Polymers by ATR
2	17	63.81	Nylon 6/9	Sprouse Polymers by ATR
3	290	62.79	Poly(amide-6,6:amide-6)	Hummel Polymer and Additives
4	287	61.41	Polyamide-6,6	Hummel Polymer and Additives
5	18	61.12	Nylon 6/10	Sprouse Polymers by ATR
6	19	59.54	Nylon 6/12	Sprouse Polymers by ATR
7	1052	59.45	Polyamide-4,6	Hummel Polymer and Additives
8	25	58.96	Nylon 6/6; Poly(hexamethylene adipamide)	Sprouse Polymers by Transmission
9	286	58.83	Polyamide-6 + polyamide-6,6	Hummel Polymer and Additives
10	28	58.80	POLYAMIDE 6 + POLYAMIDE 6,6	Hummel Polymer Sample Library

FTIR analysis report of foreign matter

EDX can also help cross-identify foreign matter. Figures 5-8 show black foreign matter analyzed using EDX. The plastic itself is composed primarily of carbon (C). Bromine (Br) also appears in the elemental spectrum. Bromine is a halogen flame retardant commonly used in heat-resistant engineering plastics. The presence of this additive was known when the plastic was purchased, and EDX indirectly confirms that the foreign matter is residual heat-resistant plastic. Multiple analytical tools can be cross-referenced.

Bromine is a halogen, and many products are now required to be halogen-free, requiring changes to heat-resistant additives. This is important to understand.

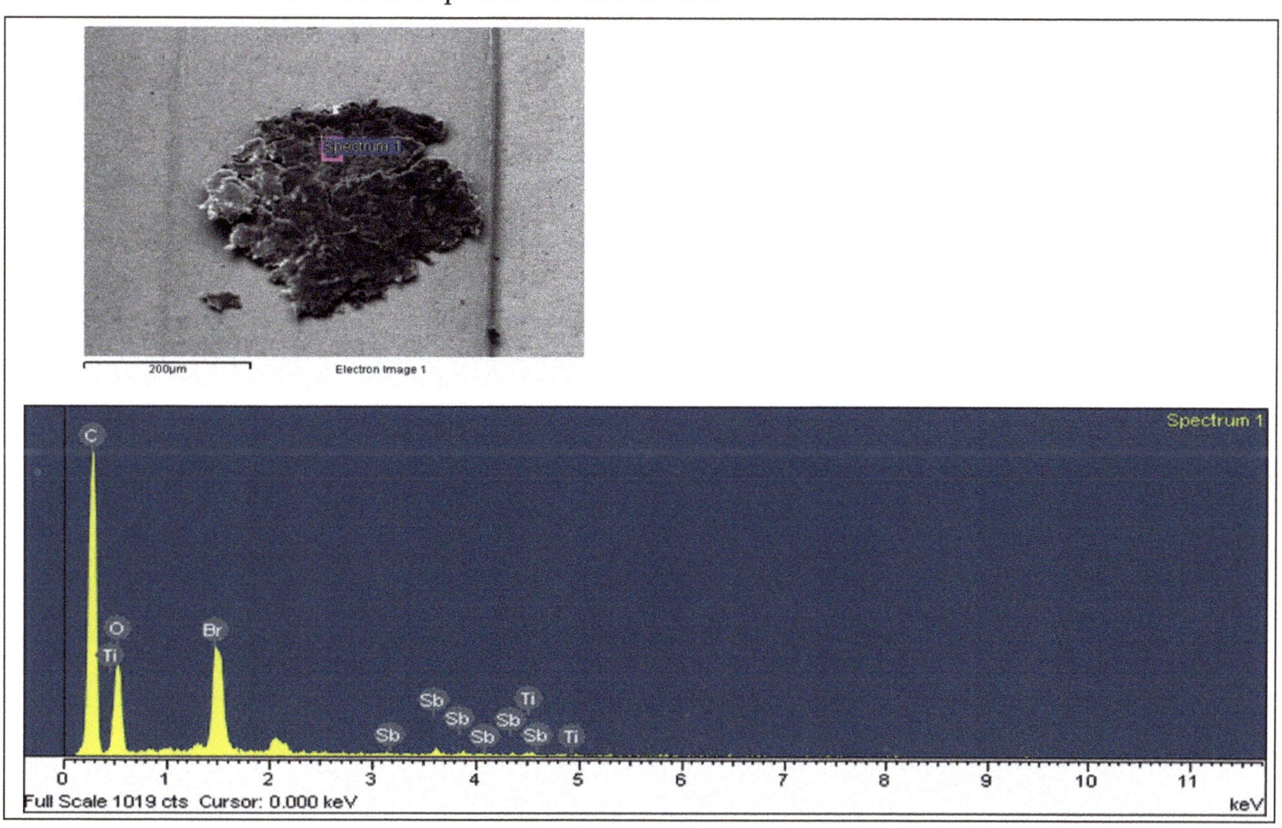

Figure 5-8. EDX analysis of foreign matter containing bromine (Br), a flame retardant.

Phosphate

I once had a particularly memorable experience: all the switches tested good, but after a week to a month, they all failed. This happened even after the products had been shipped overseas!

As shown in Figure 5-9, a layer of white crystals appeared on the surface of the metal dome inside the tactile switch, completely losing its original metallic luster. SGS chemical analysis revealed a zinc phosphate compound, and the insulating material was as solid as stone. Investigation revealed this to be related to the type of rosin in the flux. Some brands of flux react chemically with isopropyl alcohol (IPA), a solvent used to clean PCBs.

Improper work habits need to be corrected. When inspecting PCBs online for rosin residue, the operator would use IPA to scrub the dirt away and then return the brush to the solvent tank. After repeated use, the transparent IPA turned cloudy, revealing a complex collection of salt compounds. It's best not to use IPA to clean switches or contact products unless the manufacturer confirms that it won't react chemically.

Sometimes this alone still can't solve the problem, so you need to change suppliers and switch to different brands of flux. Because each manufacturer adds different rosin ingredients, they are all secret recipes, and some may cause adverse reactions.

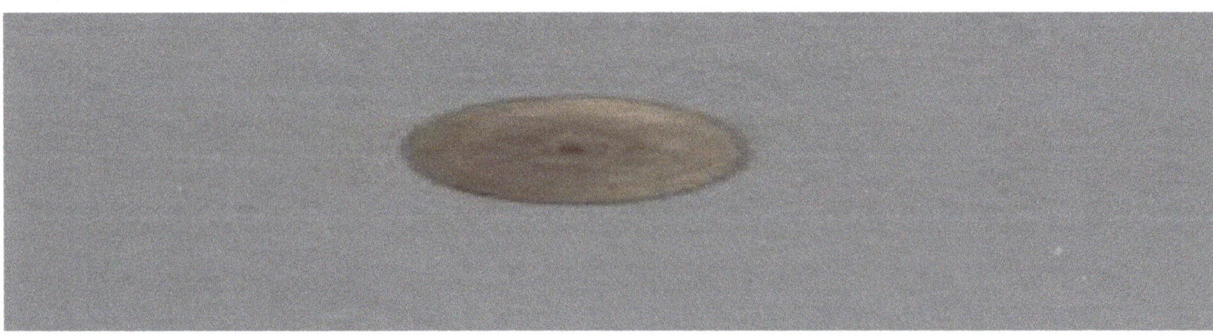

Figure 5-9. Failed metal dome

Carbon deposits

Another cause of switch misconduct is carbon deposits. Black material forms on the metal contacts, as shown in Figures 5-10. Carbon deposits form when the contacts separate, generating high-temperature arc sparks that burn materials in their path, such as grease and powder, into carbon. Solutions include cleaning the parts to remove lubricants and release agents added during stamping or injection molding, maintaining a clean environment and process, and, if necessary, adding contact lubricant to the switch.

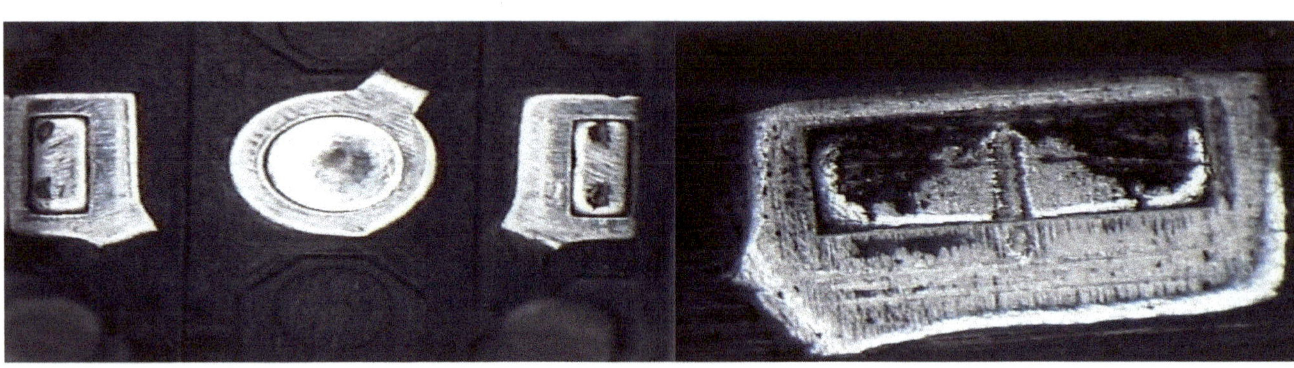

Figure 5-10. Carbon deposition at contact points

Oil pollution

Oil can sometimes get into switches, causing poor contact. See photos of this case in Figures 5-11. The source of the oil contamination? It turns out it's the mold insulation oil. The oil lines must be removed during mold changes, and the technicians don't properly handle them, leaving the molds often contaminated with oil. On some injection molding machines, you can even see unwiped oil pools. This oil can enter the product through the mold's ejector mechanism. If the machine isn't cleaned properly, the impossible can happen. Oil can cause poor contact and continuity. The photos show actual problems that have occurred.

Figure 5-11. Oil infiltration causes poor contact

Patina

Patina is formed by the oxidation of metallic copper. When the copper surface is exposed to air, oxygen, carbon dioxide, water, and salt react with the copper to form a patina. Damage or scratches to the coating expose the metallic copper, leading to the formation of patinas . The color varies from green to blue depending on the chemical compounds used.

Solutions include improving the protective coating, adding nickel + tin, silver, or gold plating, and replacing the metal dome material with stainless steel. Commercially, copper is used to reduce costs, so the ultimate decision on which improvement to make depends on cost and intended use.

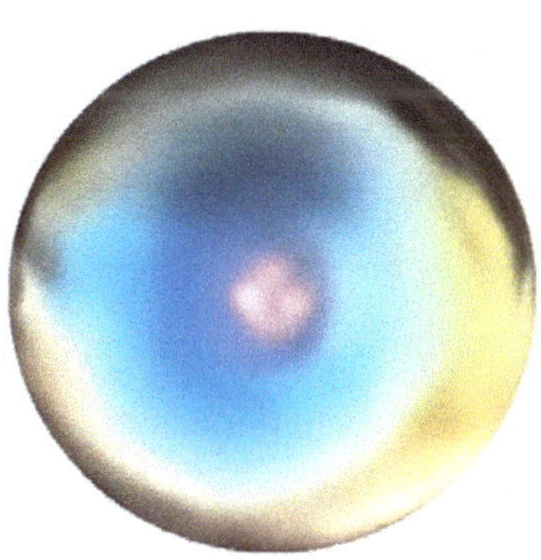

Figure 5-12. Copper shrapnel produces patina

Tactile switch high actuation force failure

Customer feedback: Only two of the seven buttons on the dishwasher panel work properly. The others require extreme pressure, or even extreme force, to operate. Previously, we discussed issues such as sulfation, fluid infiltration, plastic shavings, phosphate crystals, and foreign matter. If the switch is clean and the user has used it for a while before the problem occurs, we should investigate the user's excessive pressure. If the switch is new, we should investigate the manufacturer's fault.

The tactile switch has three fixed metal contacts. The edges of the metal dome are supported by rectangular contacts, as shown in Figure 5-13. When pressed, the center of the metal dome deforms and concaves, creating electrical conduction. The central fixed contact is structurally lower by 0-0.03mm than the rectangular contacts on either side. After deformation, the metal dome contacts precisely contact the central contacts, creating conduction. If the step is larger, by 0.02 or 0.03mm, the metal dome contacts will not contact after deformation, requiring high actuation force to deform them. This condition is considered defective.

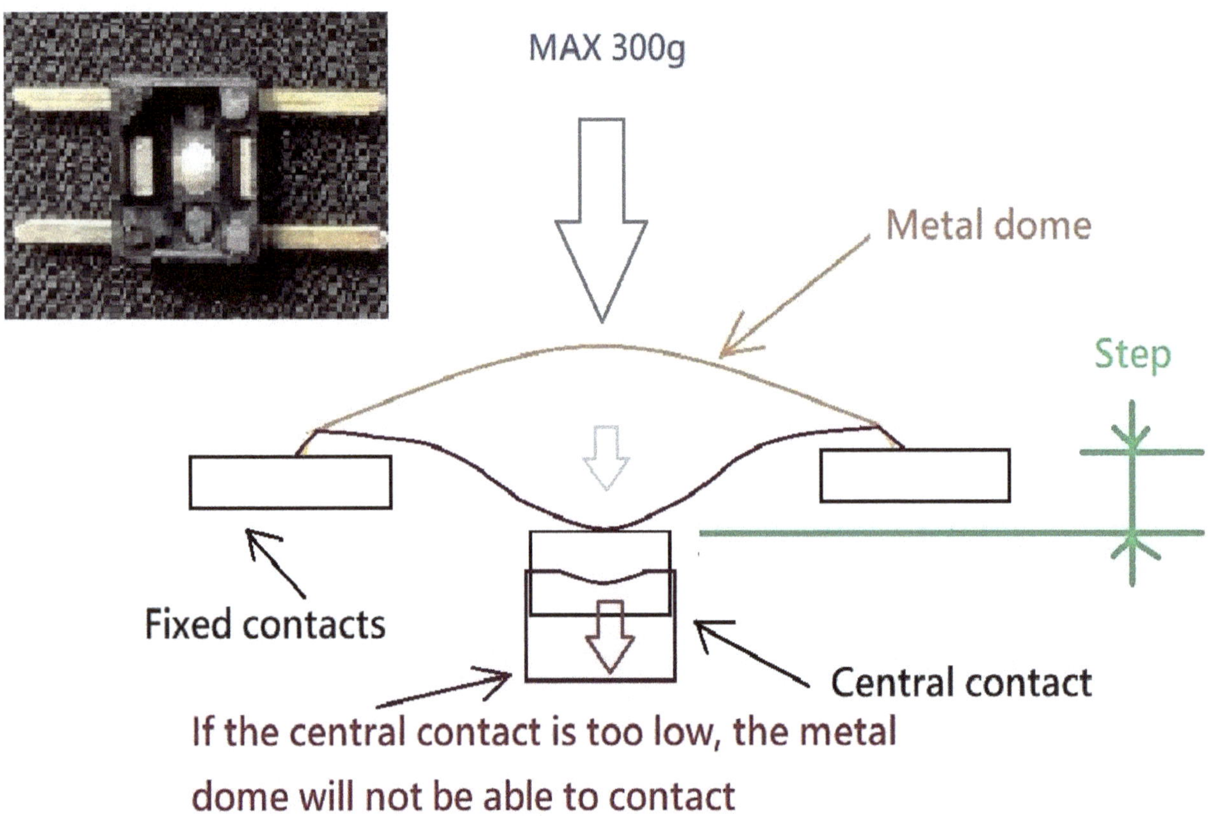

Figure 5-13. Schematic diagram of the internal structure of the switch

The force curve and electrical conduction state were measured using the tactile tester shown in Figure 5-15. The results are shown in Figure 5-14. The value in the red circle at the bottom represents the distance between the click force and the electrical on state, that is, the distance required to press the device for conduction to occur when the click force is generated. The optimal distance is 0, where the touch sensation and conduction occur simultaneously. Considering mold tolerance, a relaxation of about 0.03mm is acceptable. The setting can be tightened or relaxed.

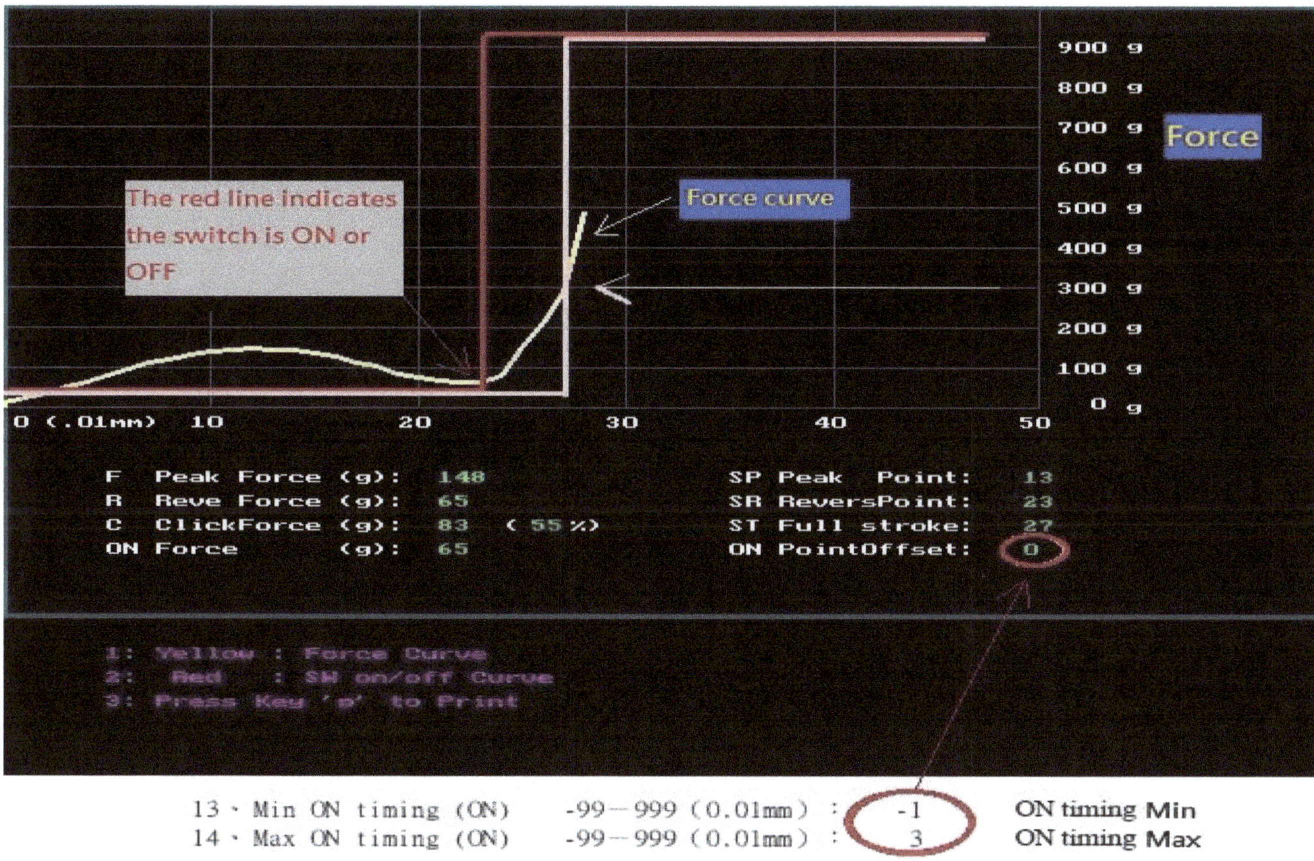

Figure 5-14: Stroke-Force Curve. The 160g tact switch test result is good, and the text is green.

Figure 5-14 above shows a stroke-force curve measured for a 160g good product. The yellow line represents the force curve, and the red line represents the actual electrical conduction state. The distance between the ON vertical line and the lowest point of the yellow curve's CLICK force is 0. For example, if the red line is 0.04mm behind, a force of 300g is required for conduction. If the distance is 0.05mm, 500g is required. While the switch will still turn on, it will exceed the 160g specification, which is too much (considering a high actuation force defect). This distance difference is called the step difference, and monitoring this data can also be used to monitor mold quality.

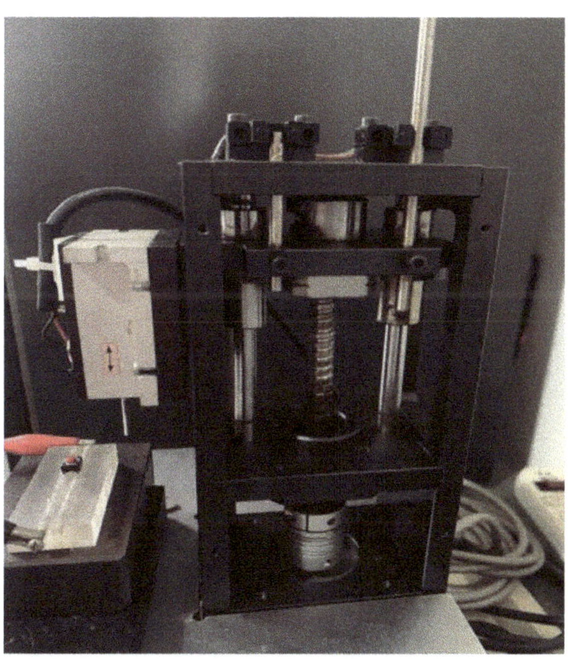

Figure 5-15 Tactile switch force tester

Chapter 6: Restriction of Hazardous Substances

RoHS

The EU RoHS Directive (Restriction of Hazardous Substances Directive) is a mandatory EU standard designed to restrict the use of certain hazardous substances in electrical and electronic equipment to protect human health and the environment. The RoHS Directive primarily regulates the content of lead, mercury, cadmium, hexavalent chromium, polybrominated biphenyls (PBBs), and polybrominated diphenyl ethers (PBDEs) in electrical and electronic products, requiring that these substances be kept below specific limits. The limits stipulate that lead, mercury, hexavalent chromium, PBBs, and PBDEs must be less than 1000 ppm, and cadmium must be less than 100 ppm.

X-ray Fluorescence Spectrometer(XRF) [Non-destructive analysis]

XRF is used for incoming material inspection in response to RoHS regulations. However, this XRF is not perfect. Its chromium and bromine detection is not precise enough. Chromium is the total chromium value, not the regulated hexavalent chromium, and bromine is the total bromine value, not the regulated PBB and PBDE values. However, its rapid detection within 3 to 4 minutes makes it a very useful primary inspection tool.

XRF uses an X-ray beam to illuminate a specimen, exciting the elements within it. When the atoms return from the excited state to the ground state, the emitted fluorescence is detected. A spectrometer analyzes the energy and intensity of the fluorescence to determine the type and content of the elements within the specimen. XRF offers rapid, non-contact, non-destructive analysis, and multi-element analysis. Figure 6-1 shows an example of an XRF analysis report for heat-resistant plastic. The red text indicates a bromine content as high as 34,800 PPM (3.48%). Bromine was previously a legal additive for flame-retardant materials. Whether excessive amounts of PBBs and PBDEs are present requires further analysis using other chemical methods. This can be done by outsourcing the analysis to a professional company such as SGS.

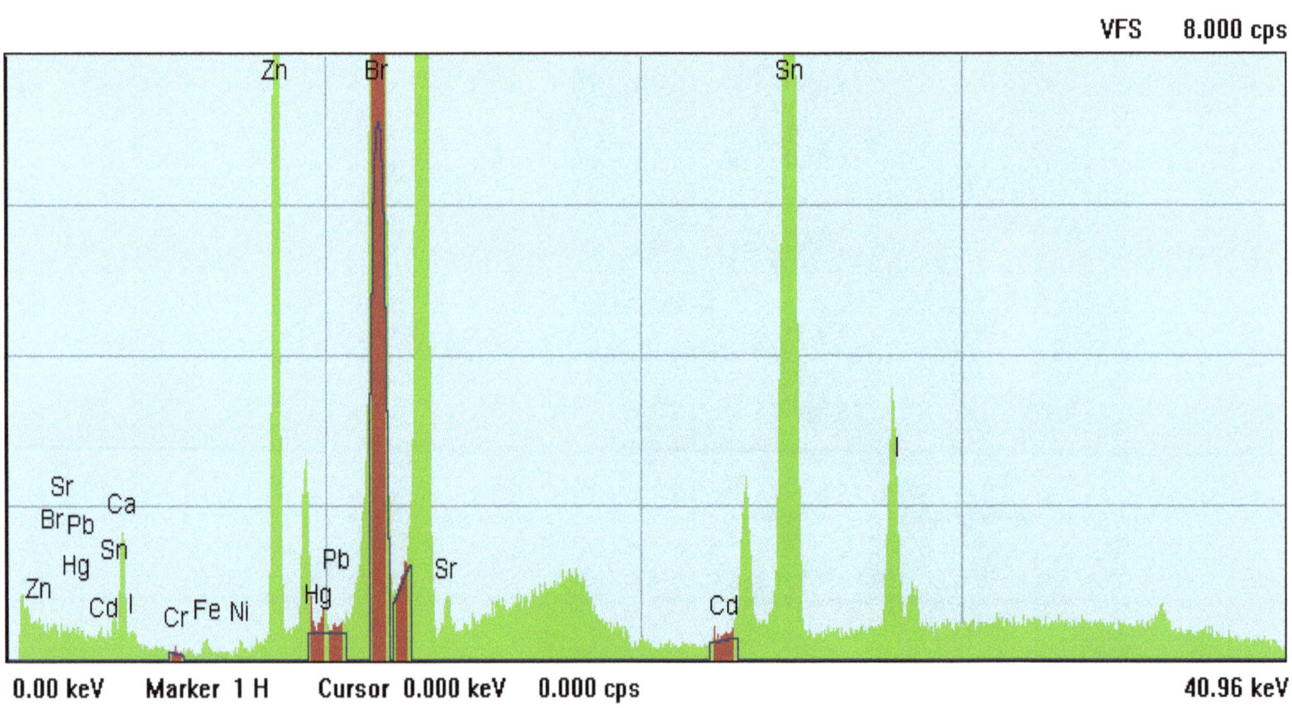

[Density of harmful element]

No.	Target	Results	Unit	3sigma	Intensity[cps/mA]	method
1	Pb	0.6544	ppm	21.9090	-	Calib.
3	Cd	0.0686	ppm	28.0102	-	Calib.
4	Cr	0.3838	ppm	64.5597	-	Calib.
5	Hg	7.5270	ppm	26.9532	-	Calib.
6	Br	34800.1188	ppm	2436.6351	-	Calib.

[Other elements:FPM]

Quant. Corr. : Standard-less

Elem.	Line	Mass[%]	3sigma[%]	Intensity[cps/mA]
20 Ca Calcium	K	1.3502	0.1143	67.49
26 Fe Iron	K	0.0132	0.0041	10.05
28 Ni Nickel	K	0.0040	0.0018	6.67
30 Zn Zinc	K	0.2567	0.0050	821.22
38 Sr Strontium	K	0.0088	0.0017	34.20
50 Sn Tin	K	0.5722	0.0079	1710.30
53 I Iodine	K	0.0013	0.0032	3.57
CH2		94.3127		

Figure 6-1. XRF test report of heat-resistant plastics

RoHS Violations

Once, a product sold to Singapore was found to contain excessive amounts of hazardous substances, and the screws exceeded the standard for hexavalent chromium. As a result, we sent personnel to Singapore to replace all the screws.

After the aforementioned incident of replacing all the screws in Singapore, a more serious issue arose. The plastic casings of remote controls sold to Japan were non-RoHS compliant. I had to apologize to the Japanese customer repeatedly, saying that all inventory had to be scrapped and remade with new materials to resolve the issue. A few days later, the customer inspected the improved product, which was still defective and accused us of trying to get away with it. One can vaguely imagine the Japanese inspector's smug smile after successfully intercepting it.

Defective products returned from Japan were found to contain old plastic casings. Several old plastic casings were secretly stored on the production line, and any scratched or defective products were immediately replaced, indicating a management loophole. RoHS promotion was not fully implemented, and employees lacked RoHS awareness. Who knows how many defective products were mixed in? We refused to do business with them, and even offered to stop selling to them, but the customer refused. Ultimately, we had to use XRF to inspect each unit, incurring high testing costs, the inspection fees exceeding the value of the entire batch of products. This was another valuable experience.

Stainless steel contains chromium

One day, a customer reported that the chromium (Cr) content in a stainless steel metal dome exceeded the standard. The XRF test report, shown in Figure 6-2, shows 167,357.8 ppm of chromium in red. The customer requested a review report. As previously mentioned, XRF testing for chromium and bromine is not precise enough. The chromium value represents total chromium, not the regulated hexavalent chromium value. It should be noted that stainless steel naturally contains chromium. The last few lines of the XRF report in Figure 6-2 show that the main components of stainless steel are iron (Fe) (76.52%), nickel (Ni) (6.36%), and chromium (16.73%).

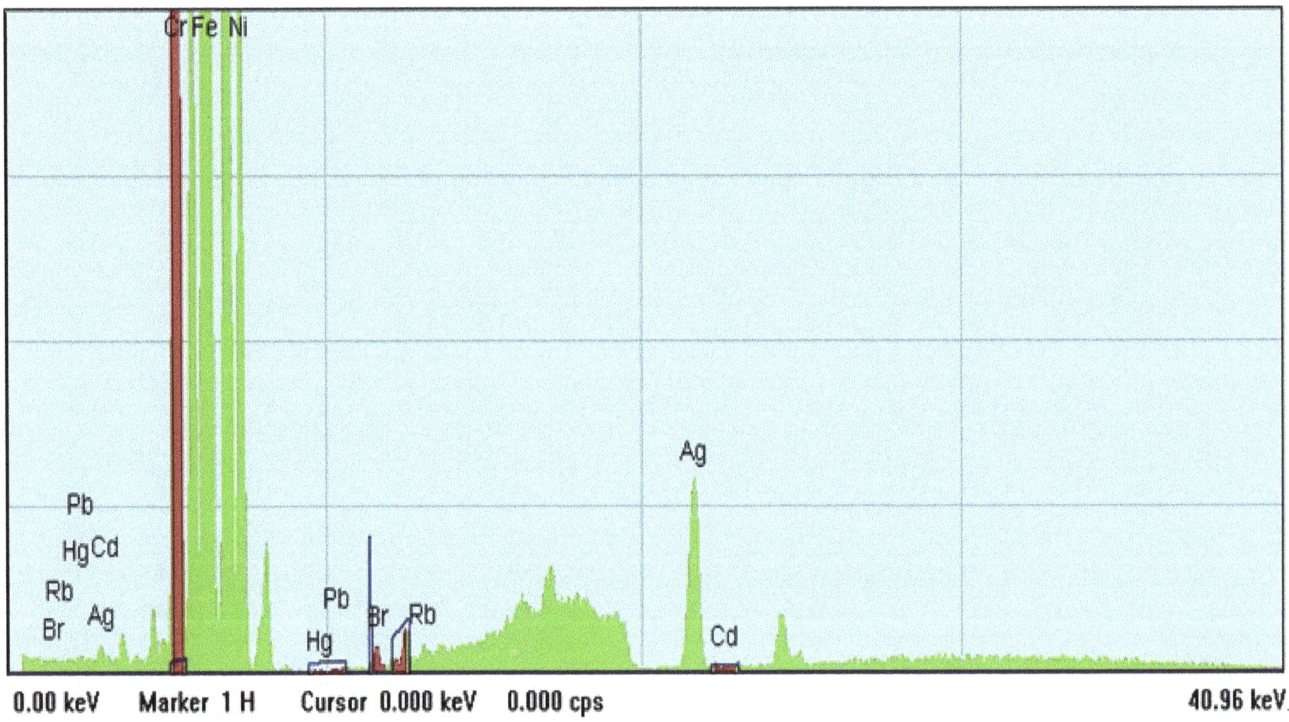

[Density of harmful element]

No.	Target	Results	Unit	3sigma	Intensity[cps/mA]	method
-	Pb	51.5604	ppm	126.4649	0.41	FP
-	Cd	0.5749	ppm	49.6367	0.02	FP
-	Cr	167357.8185	ppm	1848.9209	1593.70	FP
-	Hg	52.6092	ppm	148.9234	0.32	FP
-	Br	100.9895	ppm	56.6399	2.91	FP

[Other elements:FPM]

Quant. Corr. : Standard-less

Elem.	Line	Mass[%]	3sigma[%]	Intensity[cps/mA]
26 Fe Iron	K	76.52	0.23	5237.53
28 Ni Nickel	K	6.36	0.17	271.65
37 Rb Rubidium	K	0.01	0.01	4.08
47 Ag Silver	K	0.35	0.01	117.46

Figure 6-2. XRF test report of stainless steel, showing that the total chromium value exceeds the standard

This chromium is not hexavalent chromium. Proof of this is available through SGS testing. The test report is on the next page. A more cost-effective approach is to request the material supplier provide the SGS report

Figure 6-3 below shows the SGS test report for stainless steel. Lead, mercury, cadmium, and hexavalent chromium are all ND (Not Detectable). This SGS report provides customers with 100% peace of mind.

Note: Metal materials do not require testing for PBBs and PBDEs.

Test Item (s):	**Unit**	**Method**	**MDL**	**Result**
				No.1
Chromium VI (Cr+6)	ppm	UV-VIS after reference to US EPA 3060A.	2	N.D.
Cadmium (Cd)	ppm	ICP-AES after reference to EN 1122, method B:2001 or other acid digestion.	2	N.D.
Mercury (Hg)	ppm	ICP-AES after reference to US EPA 3052 or other acid digestion.	2	N.D.
Lead (Pb)	ppm	ICP-AES after reference to US EPA 3050B or other acid digestion.	2	N.D.

NOTE: (1) N.D. = Not detected (<MDL)
(2) ppm = mg/kg
(3) MDL = Method Detection Limit
(4) " - " = No Regulation

Figure 6-3. Stainless steel RoHS test report from SGS, all marked N.D. Not Detected

Common element symbols in test reports:

Ag (Silver)	Au (Gold)	Cu (Copper)	Fe (Iron)	Cr (Chromium)
Cd (Cadmium)	Hg (Mercury)	Ni (Nickel)	Sn (Tin)	Zn (Zinc)
C (Carbon)	Ca (Calcium)	Pb (Lead)	S (Sulfur)	O (Oxygen)
Br (Bromine)	P (Phosphorus)	Rb (Rubidium)	Sr (Strontium)	I (Iodine)
TI (Titanium)	Sb (Antimony)			

Chapter 7: Stress failure, fracture, meltdown, blistering events

Thermal stress damage to photoresistors

Figure 7-1 shows the circuit board of a human body light sensor bulb. It automatically lights up when someone approaches at night. The red arrow indicates the photoresistor. The defective photoresistor image shows a broken gold wire. The gold-plated surface of the lead frame is clean and free of burn marks, indicating no current burnout. It was a good product when it left the factory. The wire break is located at the neck of the gold ball and the gold wire. The connection between the gold ball and the chip is intact. The possible cause is the large difference in thermal expansion coefficient between the silicone encapsulation colloid and the gold wire. The excessively high temperature reflow generates thermal stress that pulls the wire apart.

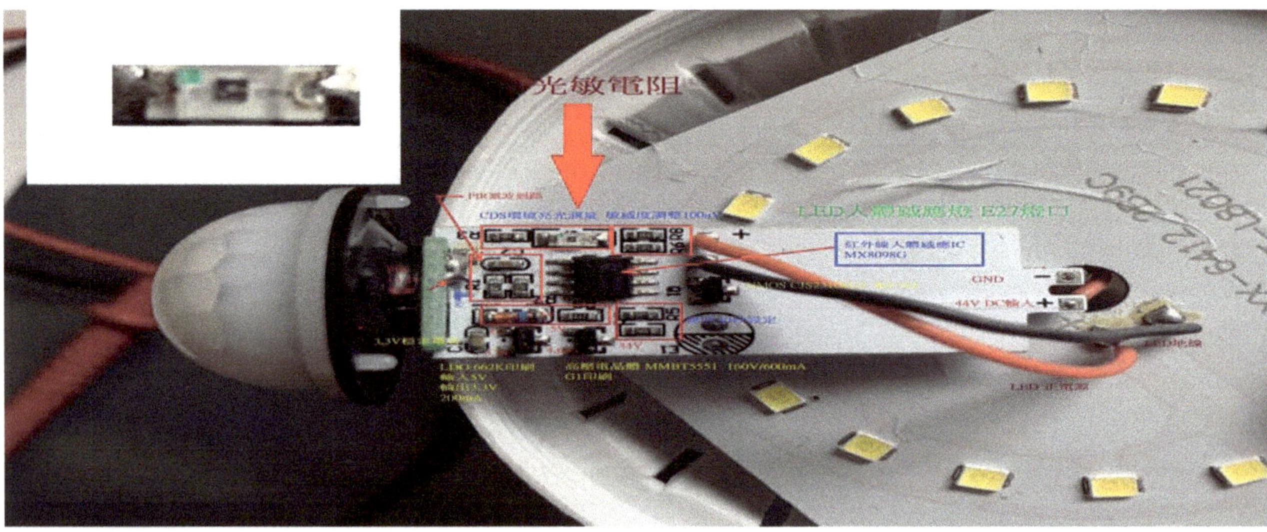

Figure 7-1. Photoresistor reference appearance

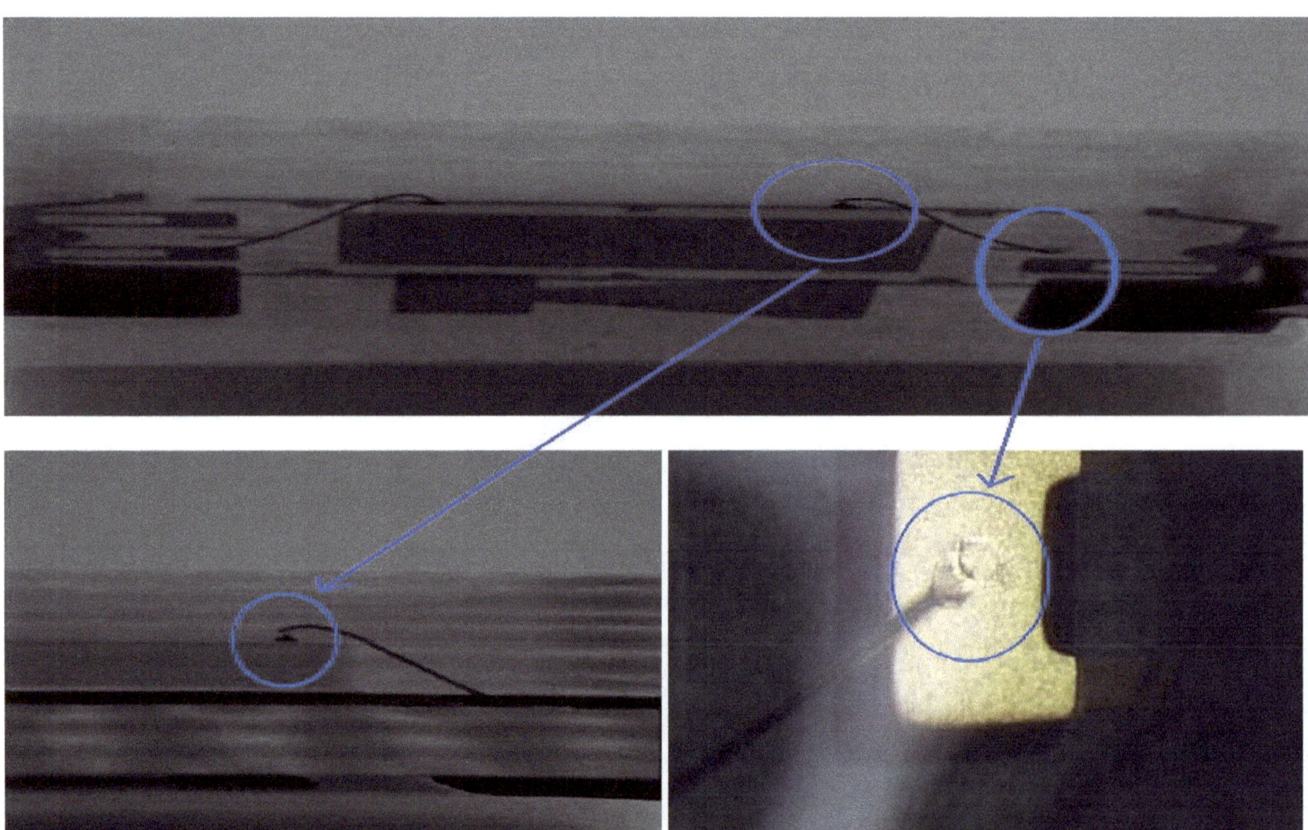

Figure 7-2. X-ray image and optical magnification image

Chip parts stress failure

Chips come in many varieties, including resistors, capacitors, inductors, etc., with various package sizes such as 0201, 0402, and 0806. The small 0201 is the most prone to problems. A crack is clearly visible at the lower right corner of the slice in Figure 7-3, with a larger crack at the bottom. The crack gradually moves upward and becomes smaller. This phenomenon indicates that stress is applied from the bottom of the component to cause damage. The stress originates from the PCB end rather than from impacting the component from above. This type of fracture often occurs on components at the edge of the PCB board, caused by stress during PCB operation.

Figure 7-3. Chip fracture and slicing example 1

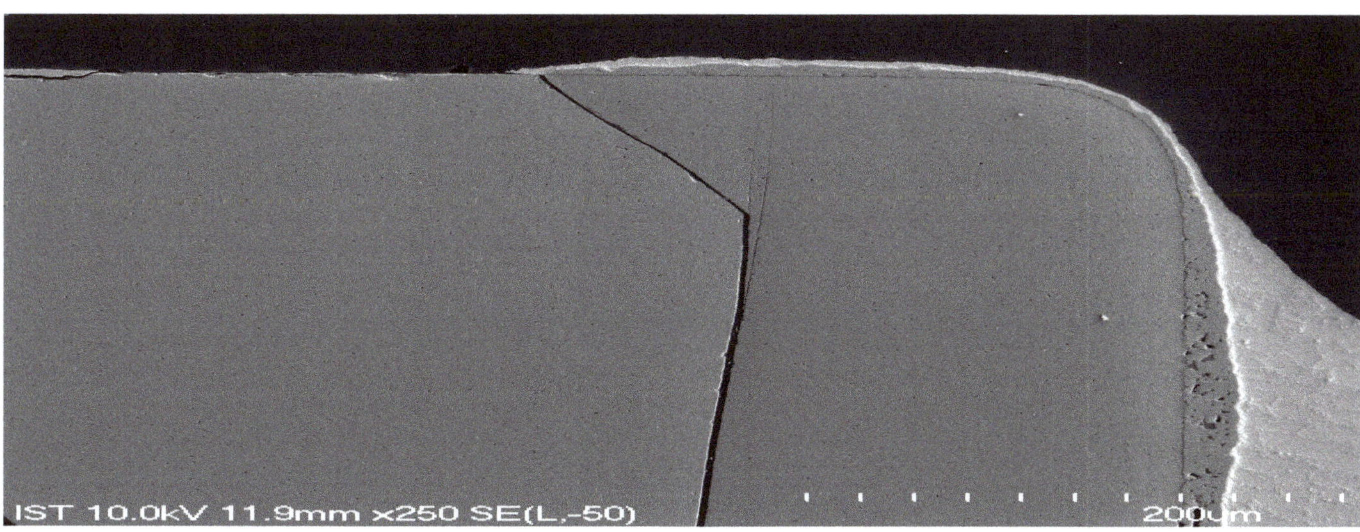

Figure 7-4. Chip fracture and slicing example 2

Crack defects are related to stress. Possible causes and solutions include:

1. Chip breakage is most often caused by stress during PCB depaneling. Small chip components are particularly susceptible to cracking when subjected to external forces. Manual depaneling and substrate stacking should be strictly prohibited, and the PCB process must be designed to minimize stress. For example, component placement should be considered away from the board edges where stress is greatest. Placing chip components horizontally or vertically can also make a difference. For example, in Figure 7-5, the chip component is located vertically at the board edge, making it more susceptible to breakage. This design consideration should also be taken into account.

2. Improper furnace profile settings, excessively rapid ramp rates, and multiple double-sided reflow processes can easily cause stress cracking in parts.
3. Poor PCB material or poor quality. The PCB softens and deforms significantly when exposed to high temperatures. Replace the PCB with a higher Tg material, for example, replacing Tg 135 with Tg 150, which has a higher glass transition temperature and reduces high-temperature deformation.
4. Use a PCB carrier to reduce deformation stress caused by the high temperatures in the reflow furnace. Also, avoid designing multiple PCBs with an excessively large overall area, as this will increase deformation. Secondly, review the depth and direction of the V-cut during board assembly. This can be discussed with the PCB manufacturer before PCB fabrication.
5. Insufficient high-temperature resistance of components is attributed to defective materials. Sometimes, switching manufacturers or using Japanese materials can improve the situation.
6. Others: Improper force applied by the test fixture, improper screw tightening operation, screw tightening drill bit slipping or PCB falling, impact during transportation, etc.

Figure 7-5. Chip fracture at the edge of the board

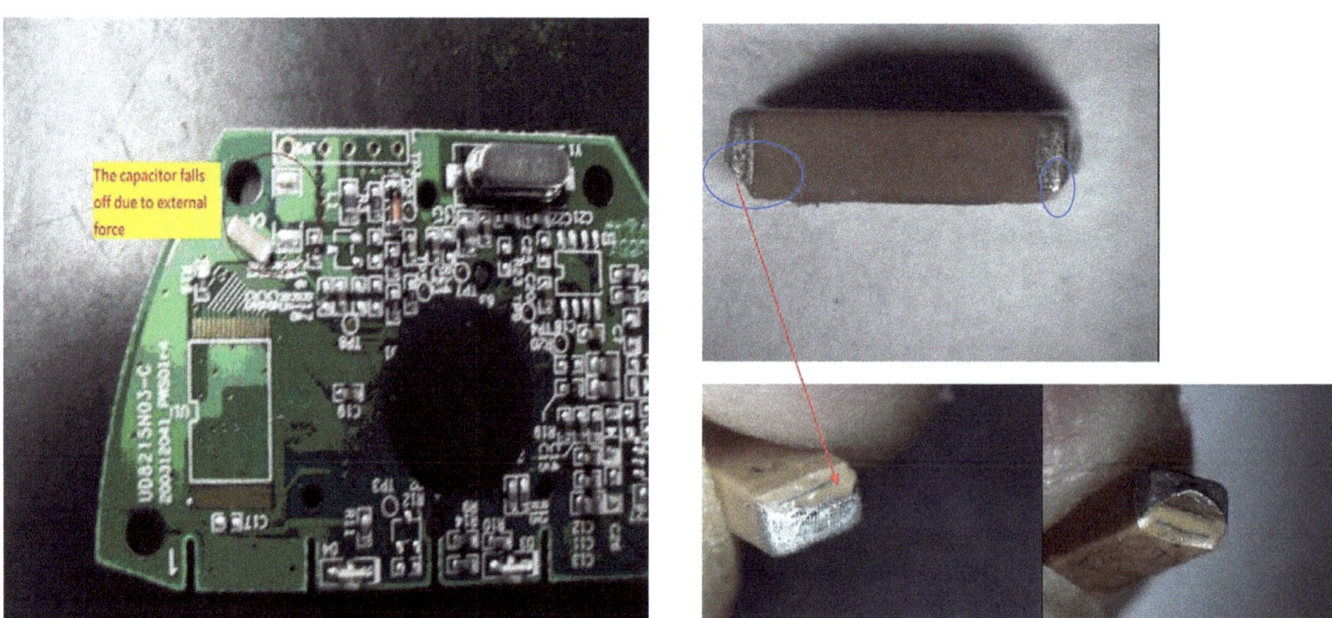

Figure 7-6. Vertical board edges and screw holes are most likely to be affected by stress. The figure shows a capacitor cracked due to stress.

LED Popcorn Stress Damage

The popcorn effect primarily occurs when moisture penetrates the component package. At 260°C in the SMT reflow oven, the water vapor rapidly evaporates, increasing the water vapor pressure from 10 ATM to 34 ATM. The resulting vapor burst causes cracks in the SMD component package. The arrows in Figure 7-7 indicate signs of LED delamination. Figure 7-8 shows a high-power AC LED popping after reflow.

Moisture is the primary cause of failure, making component moisture management crucial. Moisture-sensitive electronic components are typically vacuum-packed by the manufacturer, along with a dehumidification bag and a humidity indicator label. Figure 7-9 shows the humidity indicator label. When the label changes color from blue to pink, the material must be baked before use. The manufacturer will indicate the baking conditions. For relevant regulations, refer to IPC/JEDEC J-STD-020C.

I've encountered this popcorn incident numerous times. LEDs are difficult components to work with. LED encapsulants often absorb moisture, especially silicone, which is the worst.

Epoxy is generally fine. Furthermore, LEDs also have a one-year shelf life. If left unused for extended periods, they can easily develop cold soldering. If you can't effectively bake them yourself, you can ask the manufacturer to take them back and fix them for you. Don't forget to use this method.

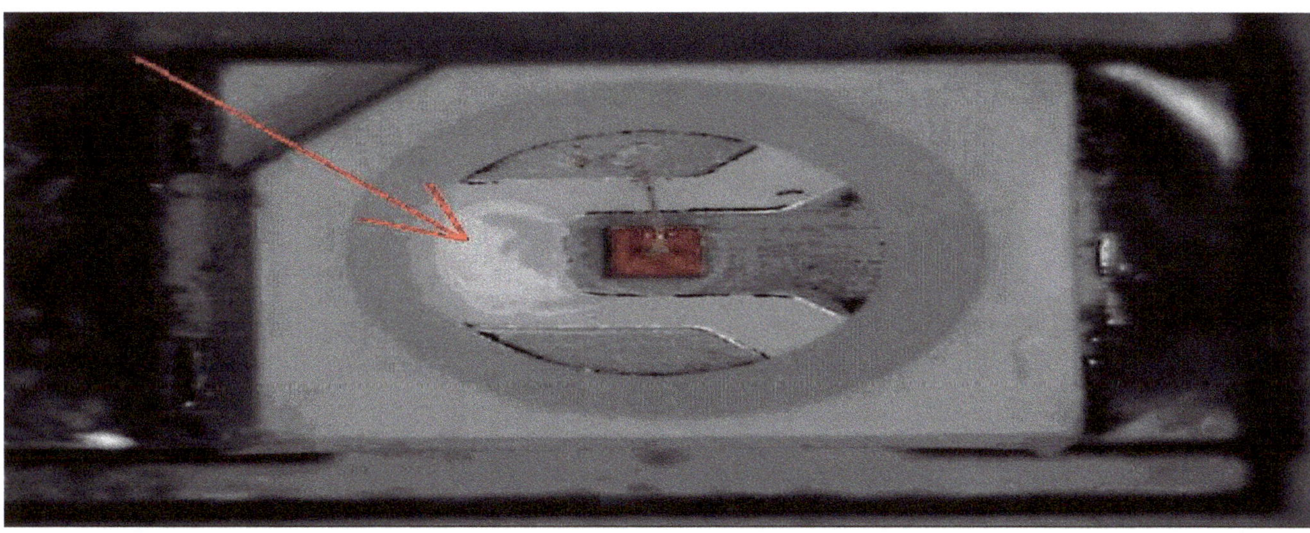

Figure 7-7. LED popcorn effect

Figure 7-8. AC LED Popcorn Effect

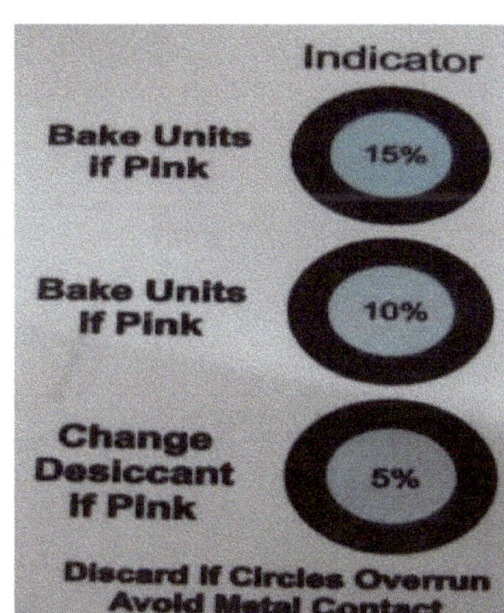

Figure 7-9. Humidity Indicator Label

Scanning acoustic microscope (C-SAM) [Classification: Non-destructive analysis]

Another tool for analyzing the popcorn phenomenon in electronic components is ultrasonic testing. Ultrasonic testing is a non-destructive method that uses the ability of ultrasound to penetrate objects of a certain thickness. By measuring the velocity of the reflected sound waves, the device can detect any structural variations within the component. When a crack is present within the object under test, the ultrasound waves will reflect at varying speeds as they pass through the air between the cracks. By collecting these reflected sound velocity values, the crack's location can be determined. Ultrasonic testing is commonly used for flaw detection of aircraft blades, metal forgings, and tire rims.

Ultrasonic inspection can also be used to inspect IC packages and internal chips for delamination or cracks. Delamination and crack defects are caused by moisture absorption. When the IC undergoes high-temperature processing in the reflow furnace, moisture rapidly expands due to heat. Once cracks form, severe cases can lead to immediate stress failure of the wafer. In milder cases, ambient air can penetrate the wafer, causing internal metal oxidation or corrosion over time, resulting in product instability and reduced reliability.

Figures 7-10 show examples of ultrasonic inspections of ICs. The right side of the figure shows different reflected sound wave curves. Red and yellow indicate suspected fault locations. Red and yellow indicate locations where the sound wave reflection rate is inconsistent with the surrounding sound wave reflection rate, indicating possible delamination. Consult a laboratory expert for interpretation or further inspection by sectioning or decapping.

Su Dongpo Park, Changzhou, China

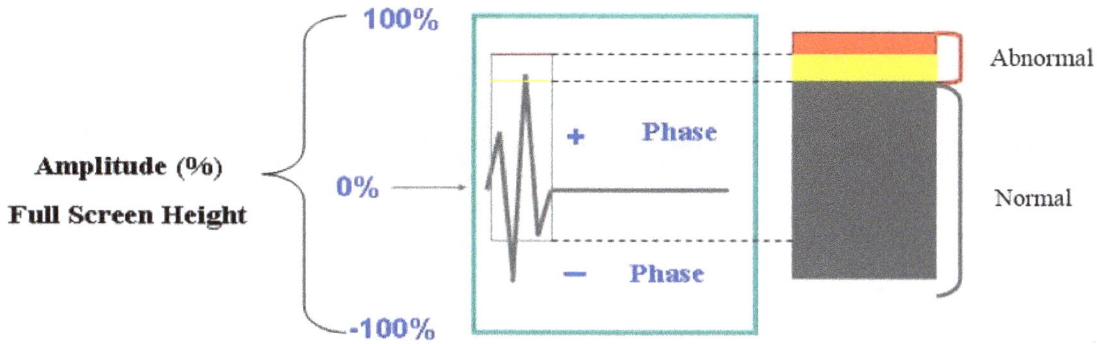

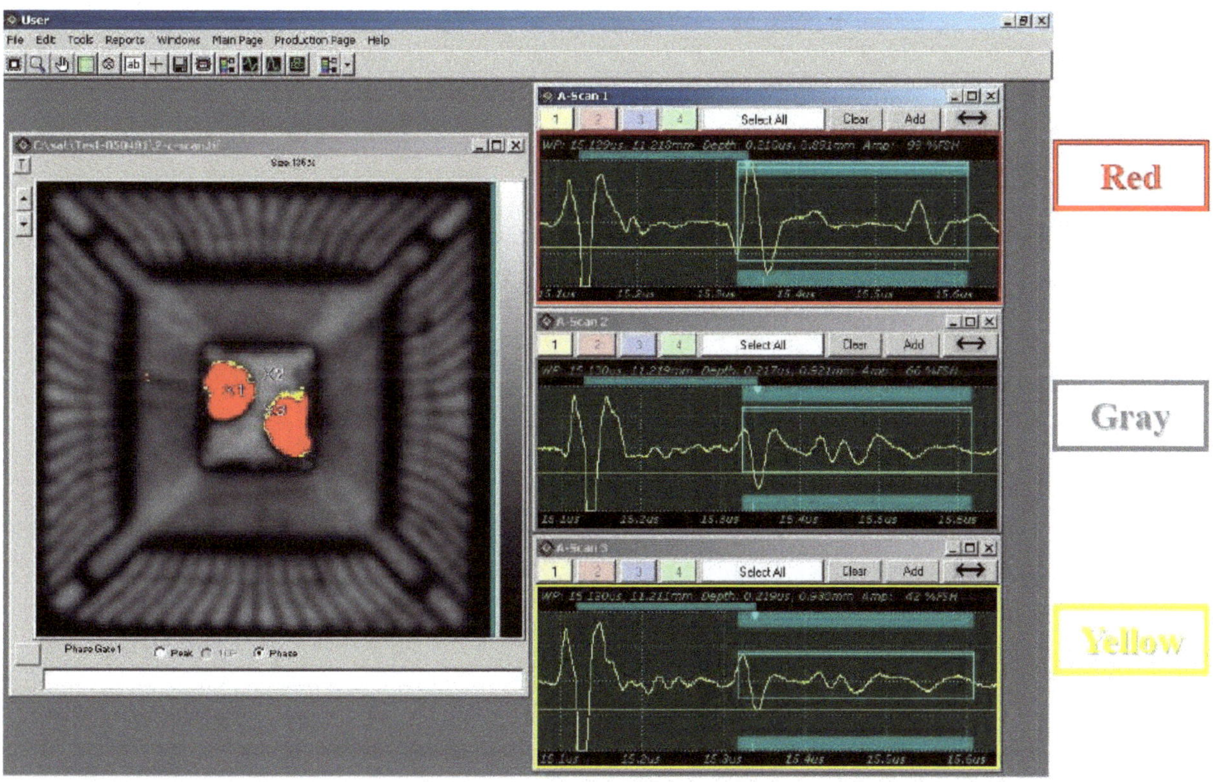

Figure 7-10. Ultrasonic inspection of the IC center wafer, red and yellow suspected delamination

Appreciation for a good article: Use Ssfari to watch

Solder Ball Generation : Source: surfacemountprocess.com

https://www.youtube.com/shorts/Jfufr1LsM2Y

https://www.youtube.com/shorts/qWa2gFF90lg?app=desktop

Plastic melting and blistering

One day, a customer reported that the switch buttons became unresponsive after passing through the DIP oven, with a defect rate of 10%. Defect photos are shown in Figures 7–8. The high temperature caused the PBT plastic actuator and internal plastic components of the switch to melt and deform, leading to degraded tactile response or stuck keys.

Low-cost PBT plastic has poor heat resistance and is a common cause of problems in the market. Heat-resistant grades of plastic (with 20–30% glass fiber added) are significantly more expensive , so the company often opts for cheaper materials due to cost considerations.

To address heat resistance issues with plastics, consider switching from PBT to PA46, PA66, PA9T, HTN, LCP, etc. You can obtain these online or directly from the manufacturer . Review the plastic before designing.

Another significant issue with plastic materials is moisture absorption. If the finished product is not stored properly, it will absorb moisture within a day, causing blistering after passing through the furnace. Figures 7-9 and 7-10 illustrate examples of blistering after furnace passage. PA46 plastic has a relatively high humidification rate of 1.6-1.8%, which can lead to problems if stored improperly. Storage humidity should ideally be kept below 60%. Considering that customers often keep the product for a long time before using it, we added dehumidification packs and maintained a storage humidity control in the warehouse below 40-60%. As a result, the product has experienced no further blistering.

On one occasion, an employee turned off the dehumidifier during a long holiday to save electricity, which resulted in the switches blistered after the customer's reflow process. In addition to express replacement shipments, we also had to compensate for the labor costs of disassembly and reinstallation—adding up to more than a year's worth of electricity savings. It was a costly mistake.

Since then, quality control has added a new task: conducting random inspections of the warehouse temperature and humidity log. Unauthorized power shutdowns are strictly prohibited.

Figure 7-8. PBT Plastic actuator melted

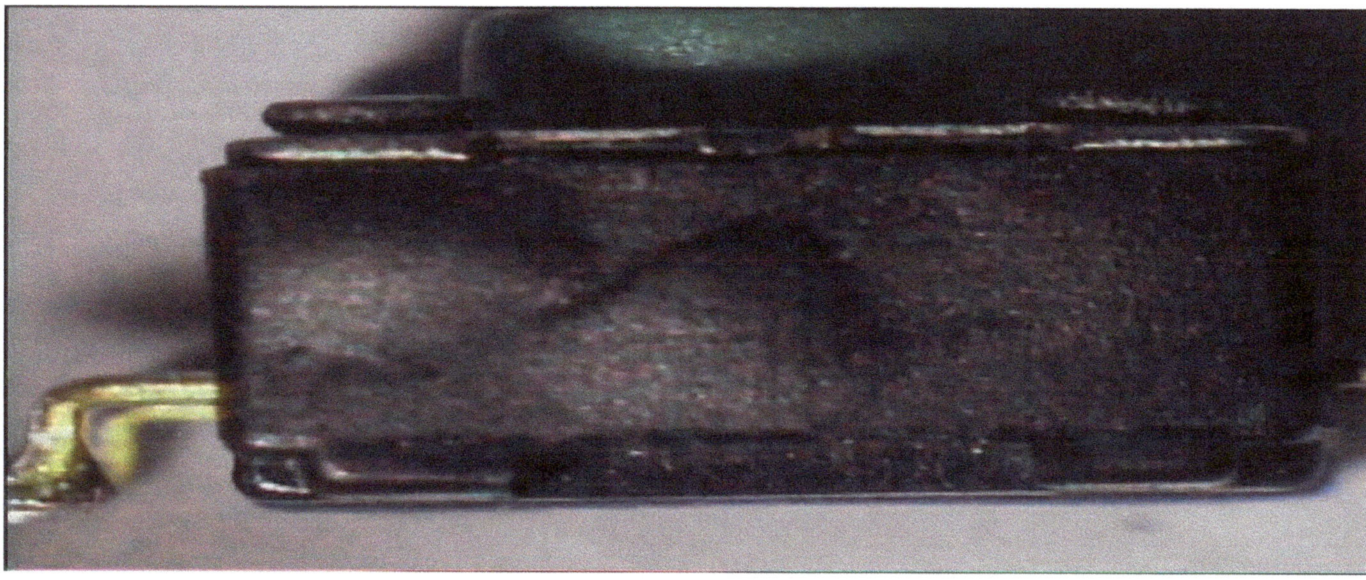

Figure 7-9. Plastic Hygroscopic Blistering Example 1 (Casing)

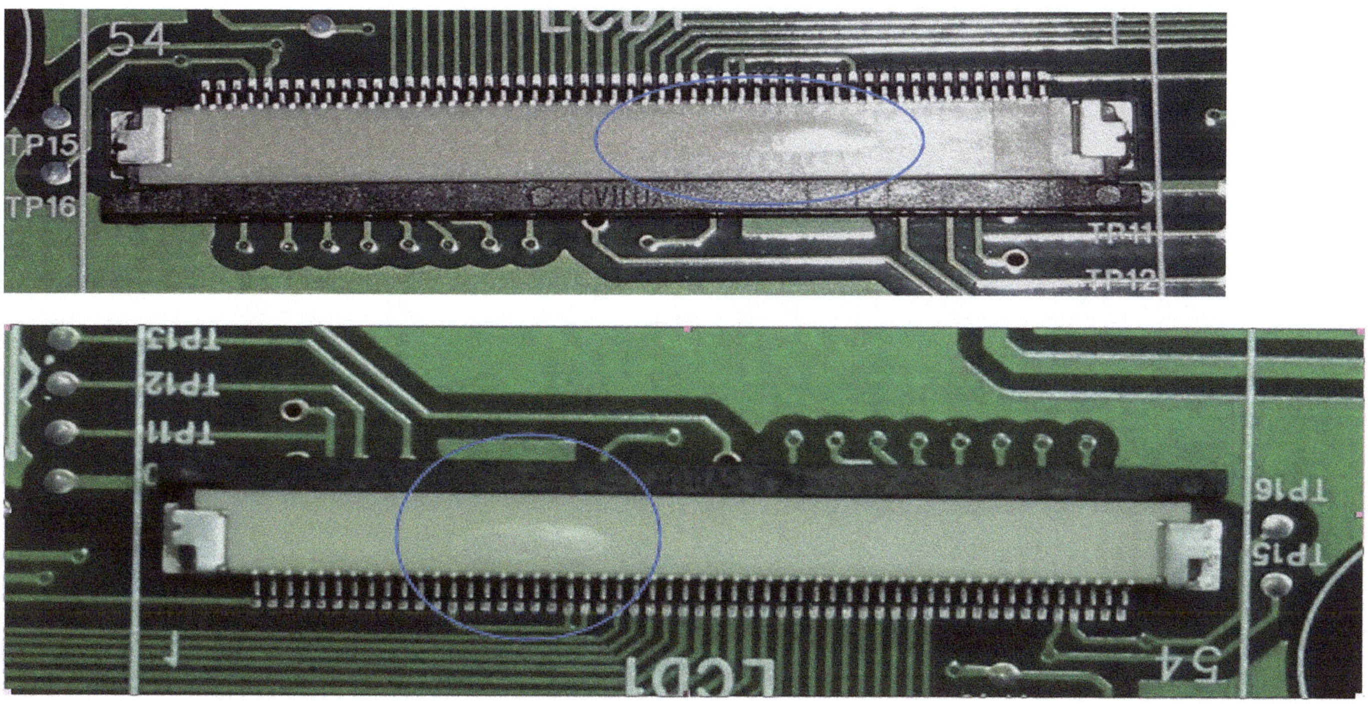

Figure 7-10. Plastic Blistering Example 2 (Connector)

Poor tactile switch accuracy

One day, a manufacturer of electronic keyboards reported a problem: they could feel a click when pressing the keys, but the keyboard didn't make any sound. It turned out that the musicians played the keyboard very softly, and only by pressing the keys lightly did the metal dome of the tactile switch deflect and sink, but there was no electrical conduction at the same time. A stronger pressure was required before the metal dome would press down to the fixed contact. Keyboardists are able to control this tiny distance.

All the PCB boards of the electronic keyboards were scrapped. There was no time to replace all 61 key switches of the electronic keyboard. The improvement measure was to modify the center of the fixed contact to raise it by 0.01 and 0.02mm. During the stamping production process, every 1,000 pieces were sampled and inspected for this important dimension

Chapter 8: Various bad cases

Defective diode

During production, it was found that a diode was not functioning properly. An investigation was initiated to determine the cause of the failure.

Using a multimeter in diode mode, it was confirmed that the diode was open in both directions, indicating no conduction. A good diode should conduct in one direction only. X-ray inspection (see Figure 8-1) revealed some internal abnormalities, prompting a decision to proceed with cross-section analysis. Both good and defective diodes were cross-sectioned to allow a comparative inspection.

Figure 8-2 shows the cross-section of a good diode, while Figure 8-3 shows that of a defective one. In Figure 8-2, the black square in the center is the silicon die, with two copper-colored metal leads on the top and bottom serving as conductive structures. The die is soldered to the leads using solder material.

It is clear that in the defective unit shown in Figure 8-3, the upper side was not properly soldered. The solder formed a hemispherical shape due to surface tension—similar to a water droplet on a flat surface—indicating poor wetting and adhesion compared to the good sample. The defective diode has only a tiny contact point at the top, which could pass the original factory inspection but fails after experiencing thermal stress during reflow, leading to malfunction.

Supplementary explanation for Figure 8-1 (X-ray image): X-ray imaging is effective for visualizing high-density metal components. Therefore, the central silicon die appears transparent, while the solder above it is faintly visible in a dome-like shape, which indicates the abnormality. Cross-sectional analysis further clarifies this issue.

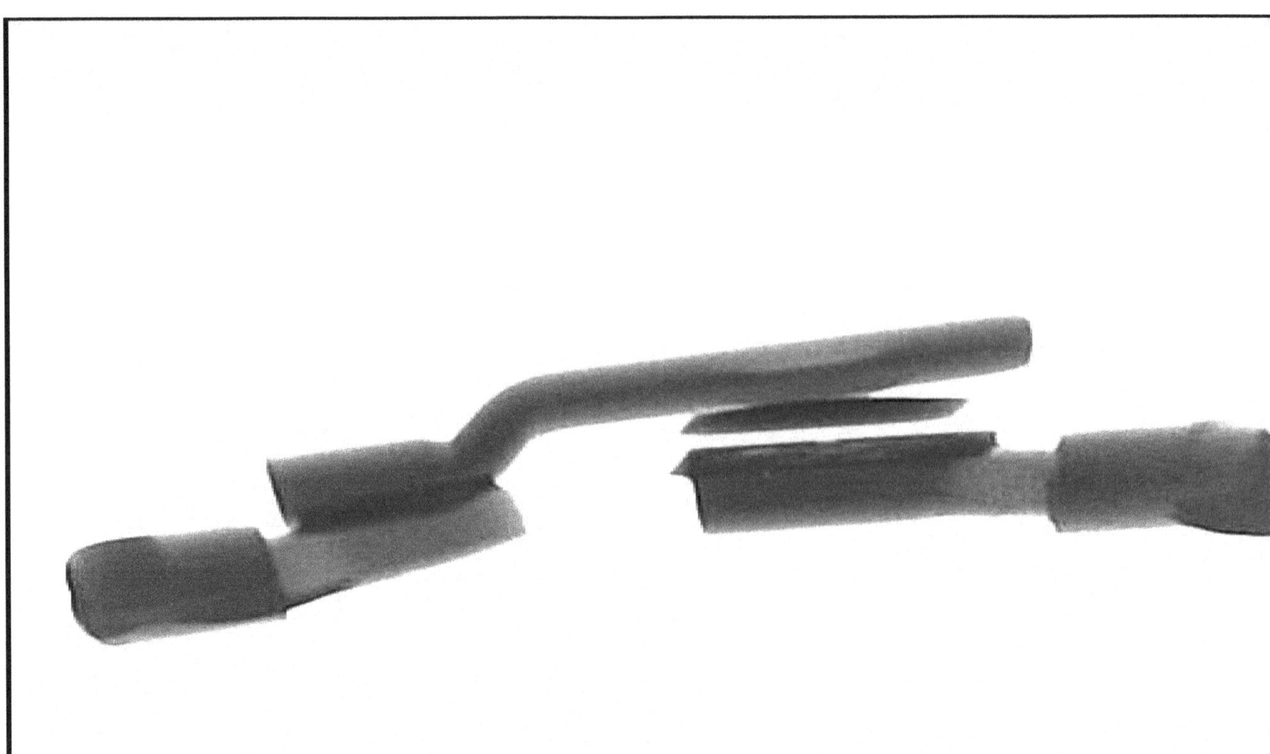

Figure 8-1. X-ray image of the defective diode. The central silicon die appears transparent.

Figure 8-2. Cross-section of a reference (good) diode for comparison.

Figure 8-3. Cross-section of the defective diode. The solder on the top side forms a hemispherical shape, indicating poor wetting.

Increasing the amount of solder or using a thicker die are both viable solutions to resolve the issue.

Defective fuse

Fuses protect electronic products from damage caused by excessive current. Inside the fuse is a low-melting-point material that melts and breaks the circuit when an overcurrent occurs, thereby protecting the device. Figure 8-4 shows the external appearance, X-ray image, and 20x magnified cross-section of a defective fuse. In the X-ray image, broken connections can already be observed on both sides.

Root Cause Analysis:

The fuse was found to have blown at both sides of the central solder joint, indicating that a very large surge current—approximately 300% to 600% over the rated current—had passed through momentarily. This suggests the failure was caused by an inrush current at power-on.

The location of the fuse break carries diagnostic significance. In typical overcurrent protection, the fuse should blow in the center due to heat accumulation from prolonged overcurrent. However, in this case, the break occurred at both ends, consistent with a short-duration but high-amplitude surge.

This finding calls for a review of the fuse selection. Fuses are generally categorized into three types:

1. Slow-blow (time-delay) 2. Standard (medium response) 3. Fast-acting (quick response)

The originally selected fast-acting fuse was too sensitive, causing it to blow after just a few power cycles. Additionally, the fuse's rated current was found to be too low for the application's actual inrush behavior. After reviewing the product's characteristics with the original manufacturer and selecting a more suitable fuse specification, the issue was resolved.

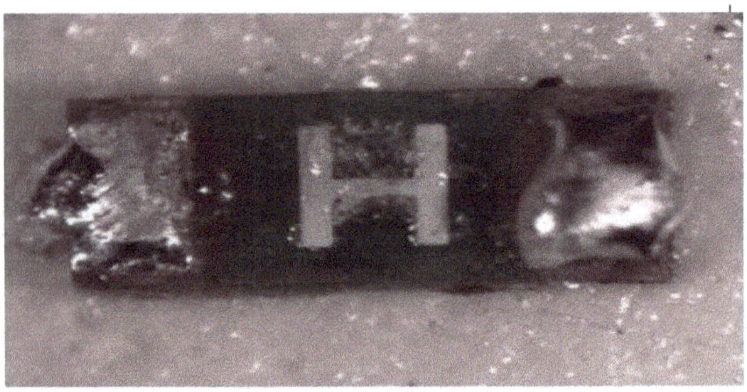

external appearance

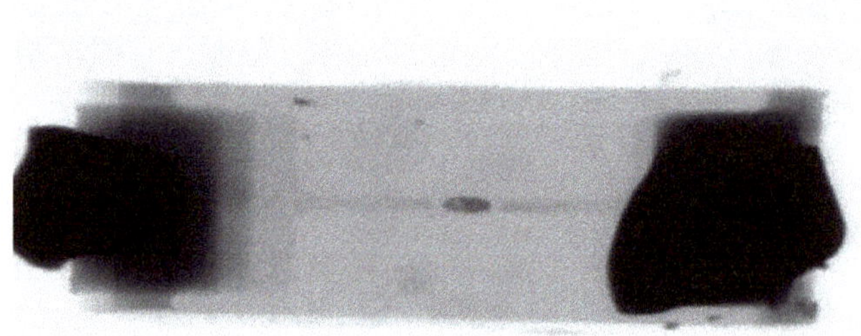

X-ray image

cross-sectional view

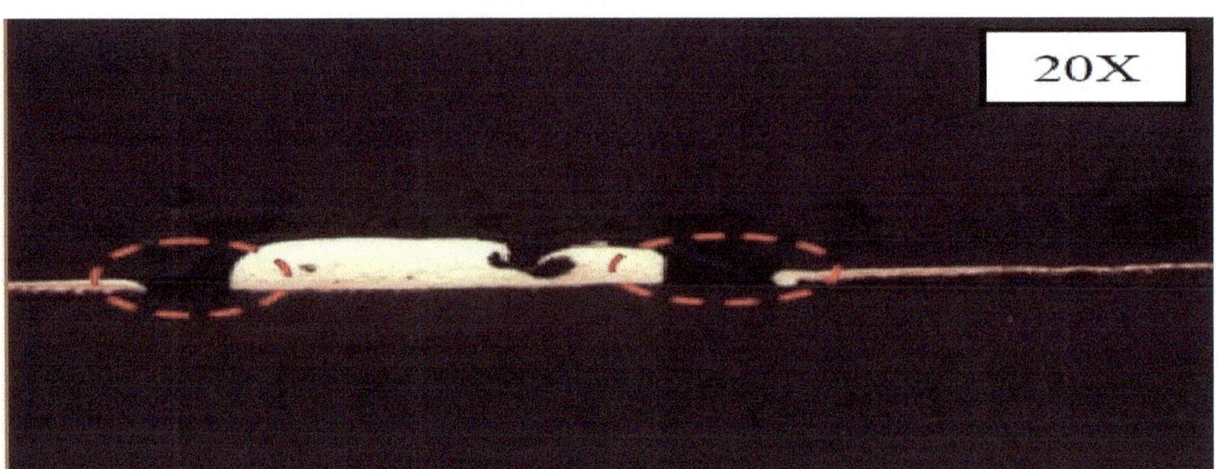

Figure 8-4. External view, X-ray image, and cross-sectional view of the defective fuse component.

Defective capacitor

A short circuit was detected in a capacitor. The failure was confirmed using a multimeter, showing a clear short-circuit condition. An initial visual inspection was performed under a microscope. Figure 8-5 shows a magnified image of the defective capacitor. Strangely, a solder trace was found on the surface of the capacitor, which was determined to be the cause of the short circuit. It is unclear how solder could have adhered to that specific location.

Figure 8-6 shows the cross-sectional analysis of the defective unit. A distinct abnormal line can be seen in the middle right section of the image, corresponding to the previously observed solder trace.
Root Cause Analysis:
The capacitor is constructed from multiple stacked electrode layers. A malfunction occurred in the stacking machine due to a clogged vacuum nozzle, which caused a misalignment during the electrode layer stacking process. As a result, one of the internal electrodes was displaced and became exposed. After reflow soldering at the customer's end, the exposed electrode unintentionally connected with external solder paste, leading to a short circuit failure.

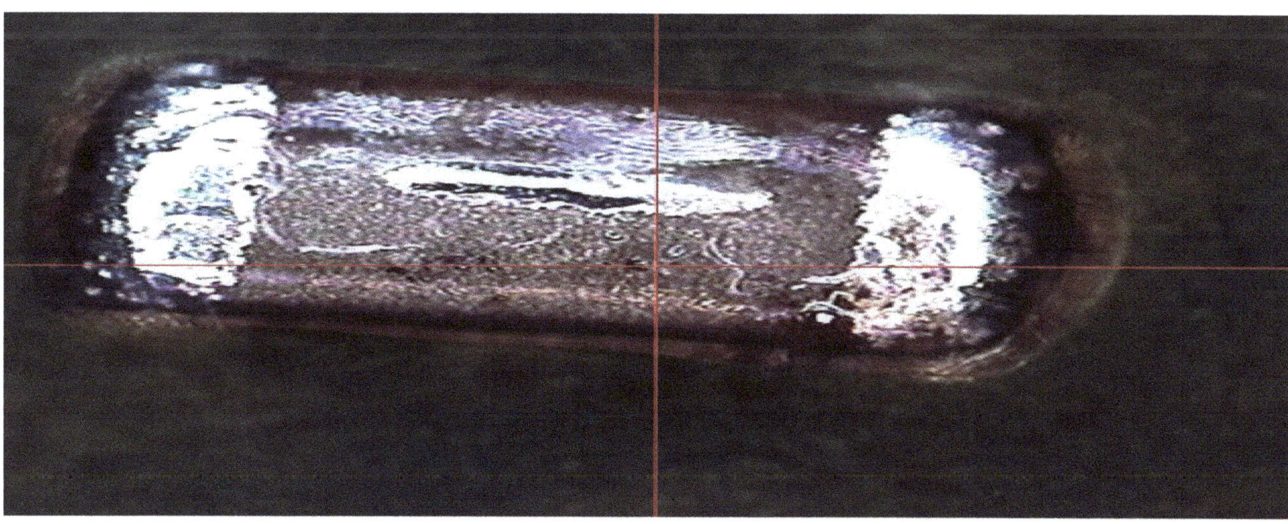

Figure 8-5. Magnified image of the defective capacitor.

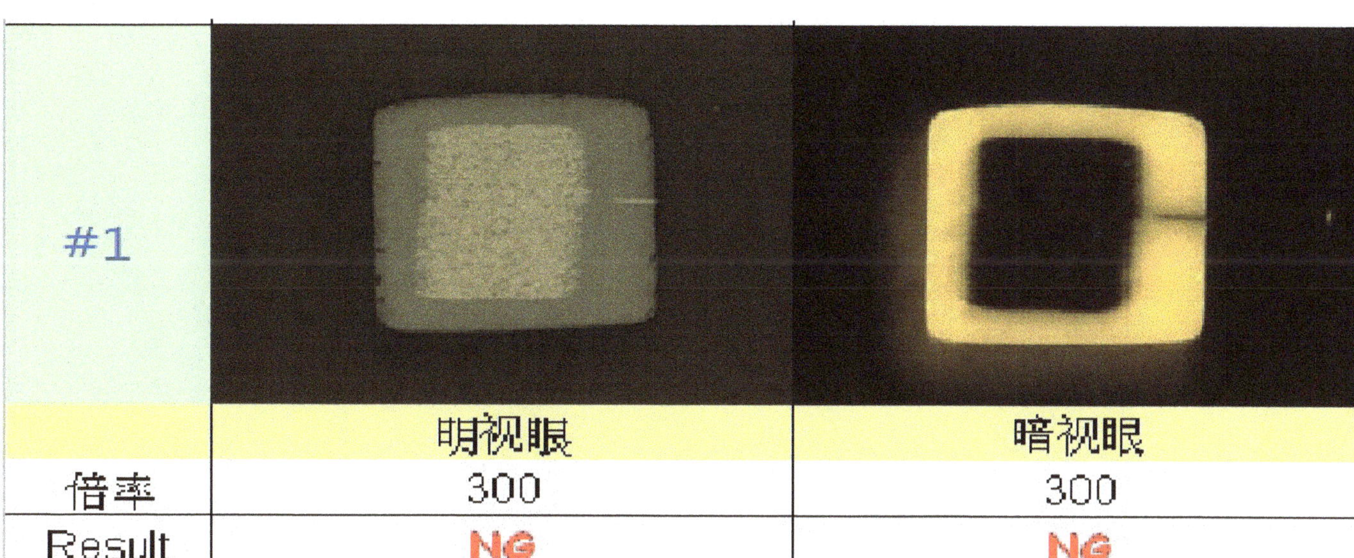

Figure 8-6. Cross-sectional image of the defective capacitor. Under alternate lighting, electrode misalignment and exposure are observed.

Buzzer failure

A piezoelectric buzzer is a sound-generating component. Its working principle involves attaching a piezoelectric ceramic disc to a vibrating metal plate. When a voltage is applied, the piezoelectric effect causes the metal plate to expand and contract, resulting in mechanical deformation. By applying a square wave voltage at a frequency of several kilohertz (kHz), the metal plate is driven to vibrate, producing sound.

For the defective unit, X-ray imaging was used to inspect the internal structure. Figure 8-8 shows top and side X-ray views of the defective buzzer. The dark circular area in the center represents the piezoelectric ceramic disc.

Root Cause Analysis:

As shown in the red circle on the right side of Figure 8-7, the terminal appears to be lifted, indicating a lack of physical contact. Without proper contact, electrical signals cannot be transmitted. To verify the issue, a hole was cut into the housing to expose the internal structure. Figure 8-8 shows the defective unit with the casing partially removed, clearly revealing the abnormality.

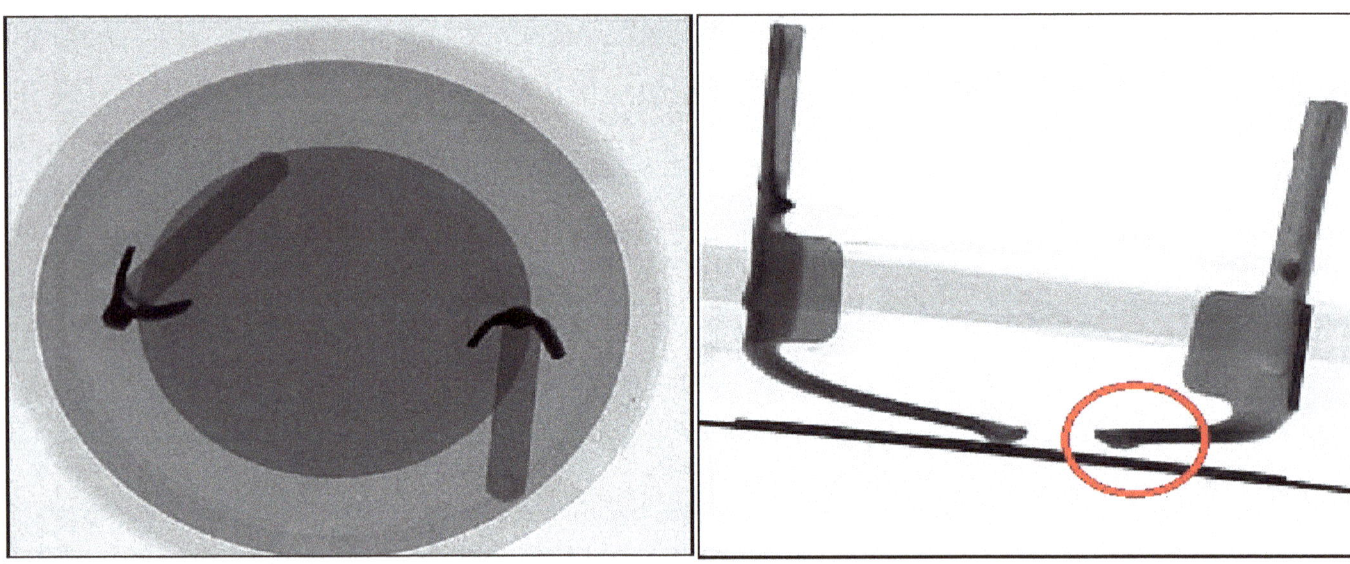

Figure 8-7. X-ray image of the defective buzzer.

Figure 8-8. Cutting open the outer shell of a defective Buzzer product

ESD Damage

Electrostatic discharge (ESD) is one of the most insidious forms of product damage in the electronics industry. It is invisible, difficult to detect immediately, and yet capable of causing millions in annual losses. A case shared by a factory manager illustrates the risk: during final testing, an operator conducted product checks in front of a CRT monitor. Though all units passed the tests, the customer reported a 100% failure rate. Investigation revealed that ESD from the CRT had damaged the units during testing.

Static electricity can be quantified using an electrostatic field meter, which typically shows excessive readings around CRT displays. Materials such as acrylic sheets, Styrofoam, foam packaging, and general plastic items are ESD hazards. These materials easily accumulate high static charges through friction and are therefore prohibited in controlled environments. Eliminating these materials from the work area is essential to maintaining ESD-safe conditions.

Defective components suspected of electrostatic discharge (ESD) damage can be sent to the original manufacturer or a certified inspection laboratory for decapsulation (De-cap) analysis. Through high-magnification optical or electron microscopy, internal damage can be visually identified and documented.

Figures 8-9 and 8-10 show IC damage caused by ESD. Figures 8-11 and 8-12 display ESD breakdown in SOT-packaged transistors, both exhibiting clear burn marks. Figure 8-13 illustrates ESD breakdown in a chip capacitor. These examples are provided for reference.

Over the years, awareness of electrostatic discharge (ESD) prevention has significantly improved. Unlike in the past, when knowledge was limited, the industry now follows well-established ESD control practices. Common ESD control equipment includes:

- ESD garments (such as jackets and caps)
- ESD footwear and wrist straps
- Anti-static chairs
- Static-dissipative table mats and conductive flooring
- Ionizing fans
- Grounding testers
- Electrostatic field meters
- Wrist strap testers
- Floor resistance testers

Each of these items is subject to scheduled inspection and testing, with specified frequencies—daily, weekly, or monthly—depending on the equipment type and usage environment. Refer to Table 8-1 for detailed inspection intervals.

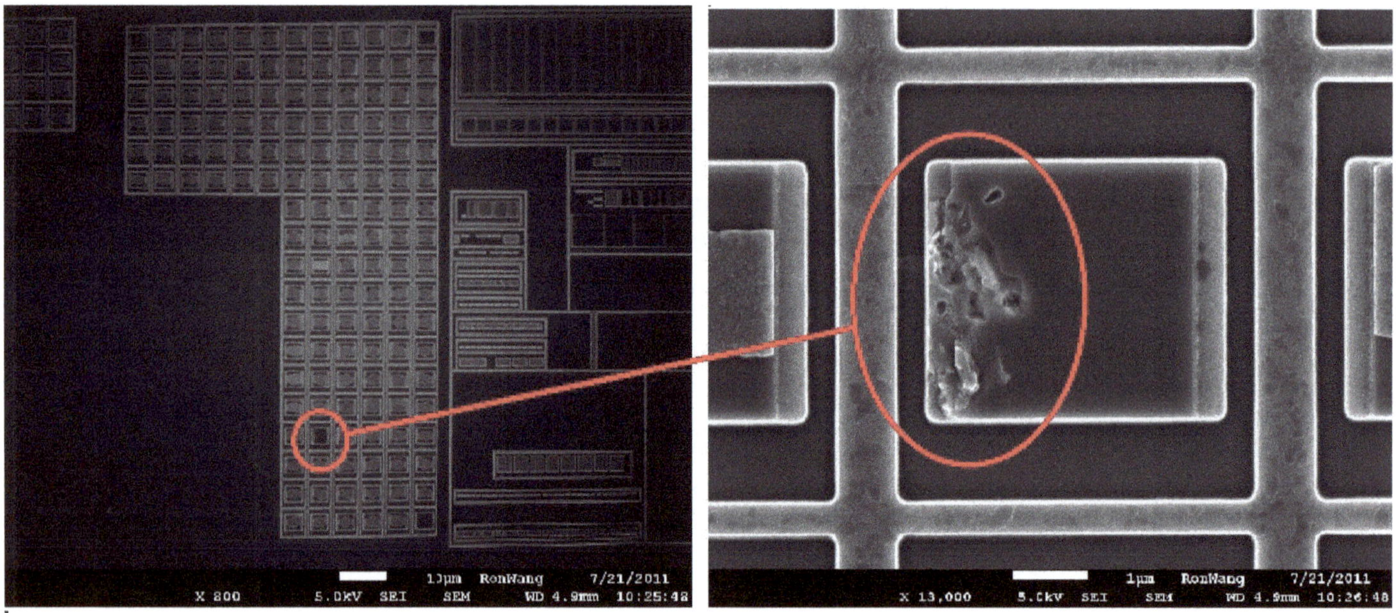

Figure 8-9. IC ESD Damage – Image 1

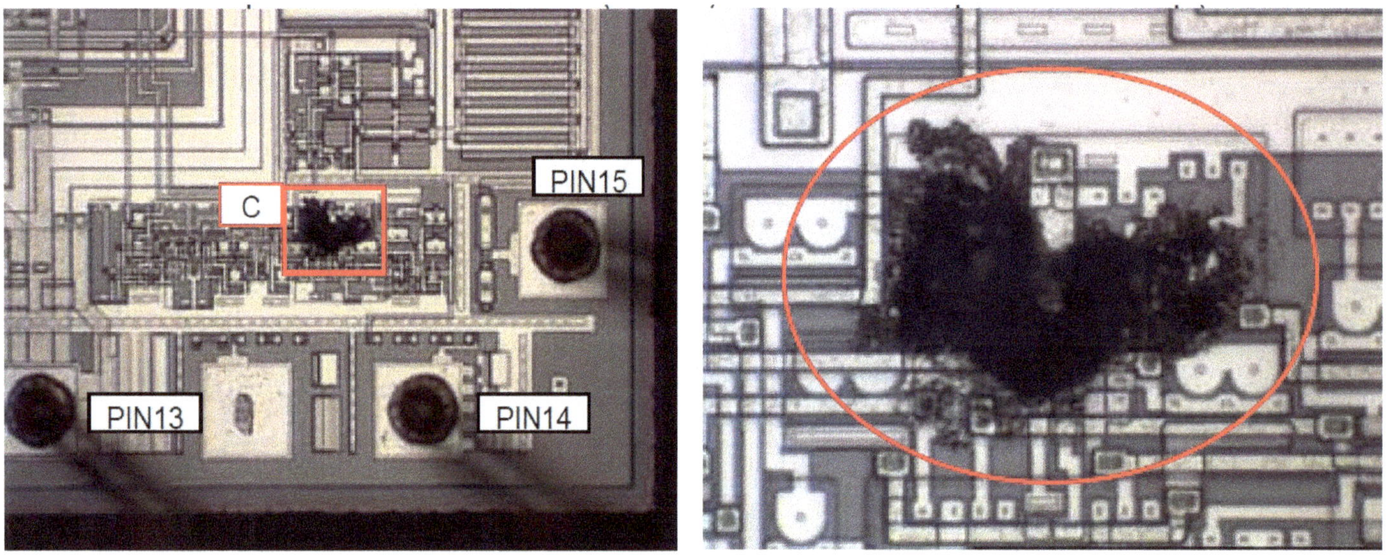

Figure 8-10. IC ESD Damage – Image 2

Figure 8-11. Transistor ESD Breakdown – Image 1

不良品
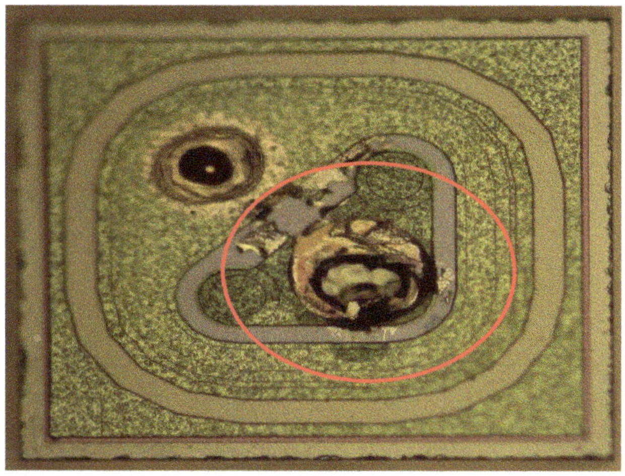

Figure 8-12. Transistor ESD Breakdown – Image 2

Defect Sample	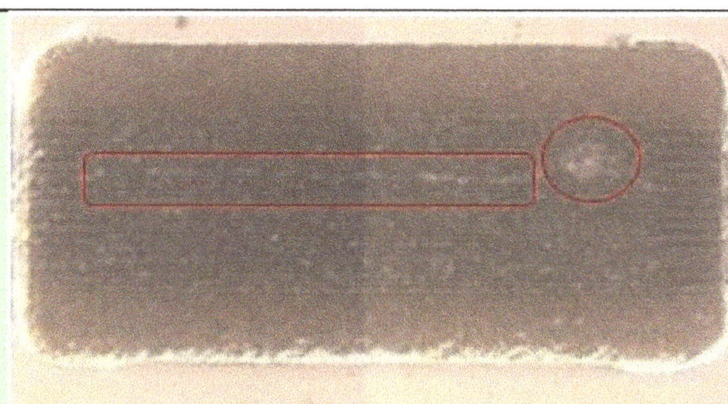		
	Left-Side	Right-Side	Part 1
Magnification	暗視50x	暗視50x	200x
Result	Breakdown and Burn Damage		

Figure 8-13. Capacitor ESD Breakdown

Item	Frequency	Specification
Anti-static Desk Mat	Twice per week	10E6~10E9 OHM/SQ
ESD garments	Biweekly random checks	10E6~10E9 OHM/SQ
Conductive Flooring	Quarterly	10E4~10E6 OHM/SQ
ESD Grounding	Once per month	Must not exceed 50 Ω
Ground	Once per month	Must not exceed 30 Ω
Ionizing Fan	Once per month	Below 100 V
ESD Wrist Strap ESD Shoes	Twice daily	Within 1 MΩ ±10%

Table 8-1. Inspection Frequencies of Various ESD Control Equipment

Lightning damage

Thunderstorms can cause damage to televisions and telephone lines throughout an area. TV tuners, for example, are particularly vulnerable due to external antennas or cable connections. Sometimes, noticeable charring on the exterior or burnt components can be seen, directly attributing the damage to the tuner to the lightning strike or the induction of lightning current.

Figure 8-14 shows lightning damage to tuner components. The red circles indicate obvious burnt marks on the exterior and bulging electrolytic capacitors. The most commonly damaged components are inductors, ICs, and capacitors connected in series with the antenna input path. Severe damage requires complete replacement.

Lightning strikes are so powerful that completely protecting a design is difficult. Adding lightning protection components can help prevent ESD damage.

Figure 8-14. Lightning Damage to Tuner Component

CSP Chip cracking

Chip Scale Package (CSP), a type of chip-level packaging, offers approximately three times the storage capacity of a comparable BGA within the same footprint. With its compact size, superior thermal dissipation, and reduced electrical noise, CSPs are commonly used in high-density applications. Each chip can be worth several US dollars.

Figure 8-15 shows a fracture at the upper-left corner of the chip. Even a slight crack can render the IC non-functional. The root cause was traced to improper handling during board stacking—such as grabbing multiple boards at once, stacking them roughly, or failing to place them gently. These inappropriate mechanical forces can lead to chip cracking.

This type of failure is rarely due to material defects, as a fractured IC corner would not pass incoming inspection. Priority should be given to reviewing internal handling and transportation procedures. From a design standpoint, applying underfill material can provide additional mechanical protection to CSP devices.

Figure 8-15. CSP IC Fractured Due to Mechanical Stress

SMT Tombstone

Tombstoning is a common defect in SMT (Surface Mount Technology), especially with small-sized passive components like resistors or capacitors. It occurs when one end of the component lifts up and stands vertically on the pad, resembling a tombstone.
Common causes include:

- Excessive solder paste volume causing high cohesive force
- Improper placement pressure by the pick-and-place machine
- Oxidized component terminations reducing solderability

- Poor pad layout with asymmetric thermal mass (e.g., large copper area on one side)
- Nitrogen reflow environment or overly fast cooling rate
- Low-quality solder paste that may explosively outgas during reflow and displace components

Figure 8-16 shows an example of a tombstoned chip. The cross-section on the right clearly shows one end of the chip has no solder wetting at all. Investigation should include cleaning or replacing materials to determine whether oxidation or process issues are responsible.

Figure 8-16. Tombstoning of a Chip Capacitor and Cross-Sectional View

Chip Tombstone Phenomenon: Best viewed using Safari browser
source: surfacemountprocess.com

https://www.youtube.com/shorts/n1gN1zMM1y0

Copper-Nickel Alloy discoloration and poor solder wetting

The main components of nickel silver plate are copper, nickel, and zinc. It has a silvery-white color and is commonly used for shielding covers and pressing plates to isolate noise interference. Its advantages include being rust-resistant and having good solderability.

A customer once rejected our product because the nickel silver plate changed color after reflow — from silvery white to light yellow. The root cause was copper oxidation under high temperature. Upon investigation, we found that nickel silver plates require anti-discoloration treatment, where a protective agent is applied to the surface. The formulation of this anti-discoloration coating is proprietary, and its heat resistance varies among manufacturers. The reflow process at 260 °C poses a significant challenge. For instance, Japan's Mitsubishi C75XXR nickel silver material has excellent anti-discoloration performance. I used it to replace the problematic German C77XXR material, which helped resolve the issue.

Before selecting nickel silver plates, it's advisable to perform two or three reflow tests to verify if the resulting color is acceptable to the customer. Incoming materials should be inspected with XRF to confirm zinc content and prevent mixing errors — a common supplier mistake. It's even recommended to submit samples with the worst discoloration for approval to avoid being judged by overly strict standards. Although severe discoloration doesn't affect electrical performance, overly picky customers may still reject the product, so precautions must be taken in advance.

We once encountered an even more unusual case of metal discoloration — the material changed color just a few hours after stamping! The material was purchased as a large roll of thin metal strip, known as hoop material. During stamping, to prevent shaped parts on the strip from entangling with each other, a layer of so-called neutral paper was inserted between them. The issue, however, stemmed from this neutral paper.

Testing with a pH meter revealed that the paper had a pH between 5.0 and 6.5 — slightly acidic. Tracing the source of the raw material showed that the paper came from various origins: sometimes pine trees from the U.S. or Canada, other times willow trees from Japan. The acidity varied, and some of the paper was bleached with sulfur compounds, which also caused differences in color intensity. With such inconsistent sources, it was clear the paper could not truly be called "neutral."

Paper containing sulfur and acid has adverse effects on metals, leading to discoloration and poor solderability. We had previously assumed the problem was due to poor-quality plating, but it turned out to be related to the composition of the paper. The issue was only resolved after switching to truly sulfur-free neutral paper or the more expensive Mylar plastic film.

Figure 8-17. Example of Nickel Silver Plate Application Location

Solderability Test

There are two common methods to test the solderability of metal terminals. One method involves directly observing the solder coverage after dipping. The component terminals are coated with flux and then vertically immersed at a speed of 25 mm/s into SAC305 solder (96.5% Sn / 3.0% Ag / 0.5% Cu) maintained at 260 °C for 10 seconds. The soldered surface is then inspected for abnormalities. A solder coverage area greater than 95% is considered a passing standard.

The other method is the solder wetting balance test. During soldering, the force curve on the terminal is recorded simultaneously. Taking the testing by FOXCONN CMC Testing Center as an example, the test conditions are as follows: (Standard referenced IEC 60060-2-69)

- Flux used: RMA-type rosin flux
- Terminal immersion speed: 1 mm/sec vertically
- Solder type: SAC305
- Solder temperature: 245 °C
- Immersion time: 5 seconds

Figure 8-18 explains the definitions of the soldering force curve, and the commissioned test results are shown in Figure 8-19. When the terminal first contacts the solder, it encounters surface tension resistance. The zero-crossing time T0 represents the moment the surface tension is overcome and wetting begins. A T0 less than 1 second is considered passing.

T2/3 represents the time to reach two-thirds of the maximum force, indicating that solder wetting is nearly complete. T2/3 should be less than 3 seconds (while typical DIP operations complete within about 5 seconds). Additionally, it should be noted that solderability test results depend on solder alloy composition, flux type, solder temperature (245 °C or 260 °C), and nitrogen atmosphere. Pass/fail criteria should be adjusted accordingly and are not fixed.

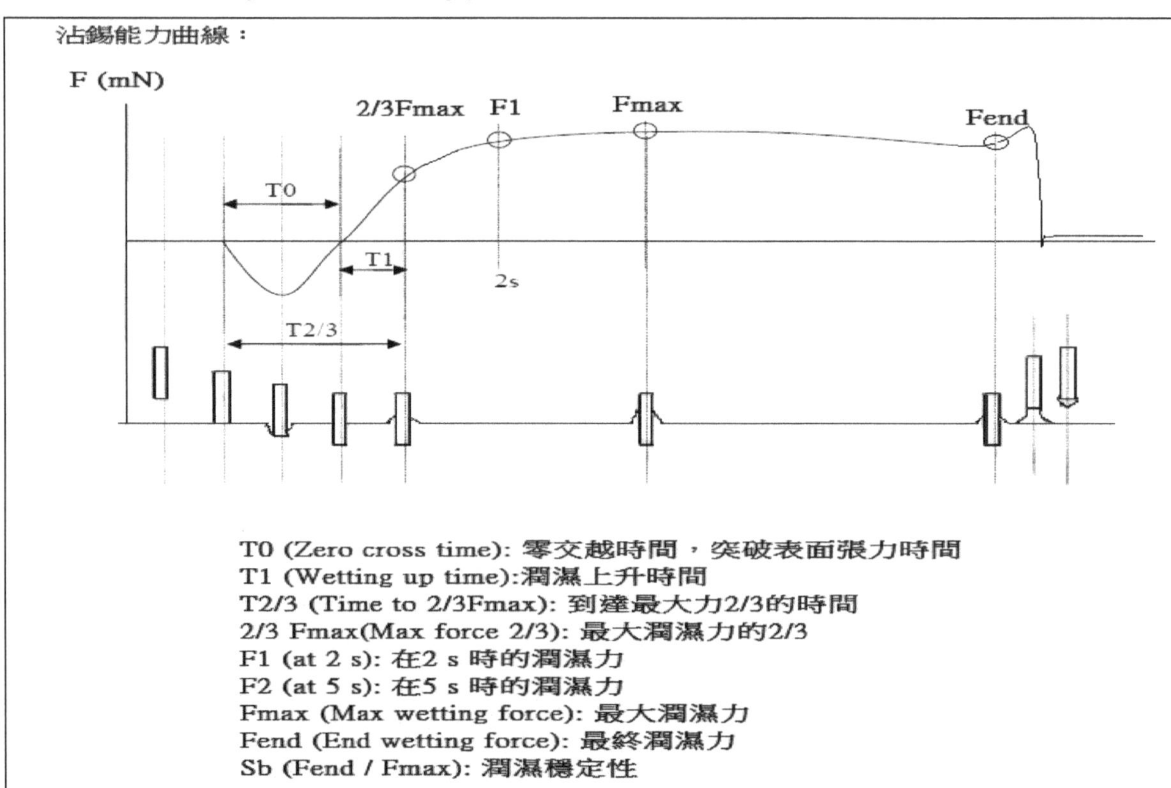

Figure 8-18. Solderability Test Graph and Terminology Definitions

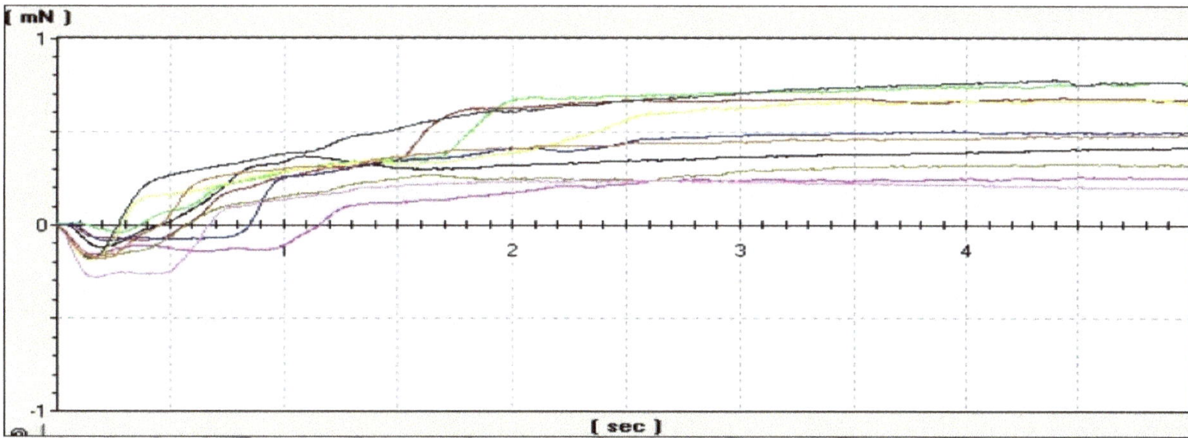

	T0 (s)	T1 (s)	T2/3 (s)	2/3Fmax (mN)	Fmax (mN)	Fend (mN)	Sb	F1 (mN)	F2 (mN)	Color of Curve
1	**0.46**	0.35	**0.81**	0.28	0.42	0.42	1.00	0.32	0.42	
2	**0.56**	1.02	**1.59**	0.45	0.68	0.68	1.00	0.62	0.68	
3	**0.36**	1.47	**1.83**	0.51	0.77	0.77	1.00	0.66	0.77	
4	**0.85**	0.62	**1.47**	0.33	0.50	0.50	1.00	0.41	0.50	
5	**1.15**	0.86	**2.01**	0.17	0.26	0.25	0.96	0.17	0.25	
6	**0.28**	1.93	**2.22**	0.45	0.67	0.65	0.97	0.39	0.65	
7	**0.57**	0.73	**1.30**	0.22	0.33	0.32	0.97	0.25	0.32	
8	**0.27**	1.25	**1.52**	0.52	0.78	0.75	0.96	0.61	0.75	
9	**0.67**	0.47	**1.14**	0.16	0.24	0.20	0.83	0.23	0.20	
10	**0.45**	0.87	**1.33**	0.32	0.48	0.48	1.00	0.41	0.48	

Figure 8-19. Solderability Test Results for 10 Sampled Components

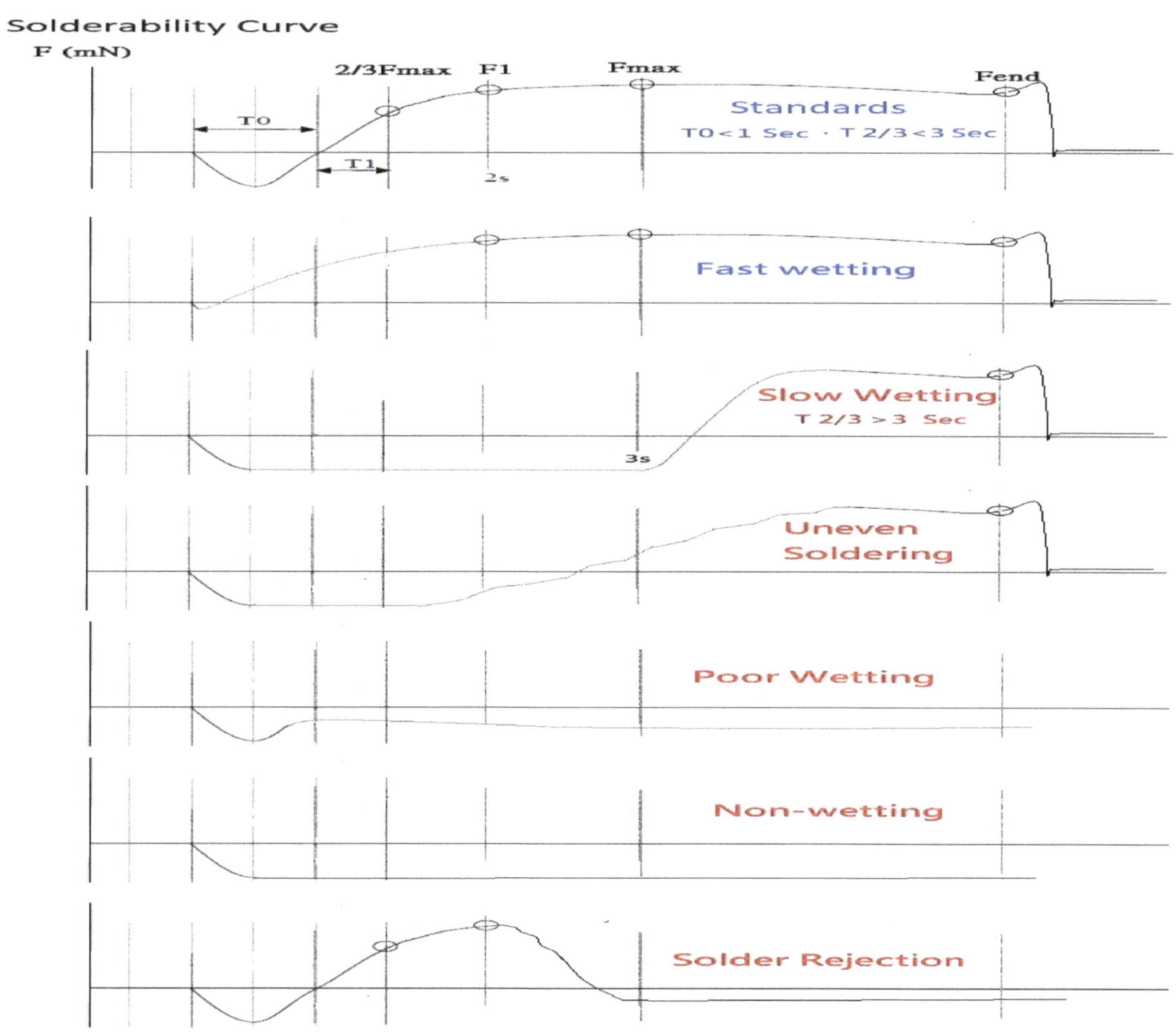

Figure 8-20. Examples of Various Solder Wetting Curves

Defective Ferrite bead

In this case, the ferrite bead was used for isolation between the digital ground and analog ground power. The customer reported that after a period of use, the bead deteriorated, causing the entire TV box to fail shortly after operation.

Measuring with a multimeter set to the ohmmeter function revealed that the ferrite bead was open internally, confirming that the ferrite bead had burned out. A cross-sectional analysis was conducted to investigate the failure cause. Figure 8-21 shows the cross-section image of the defective bead component.

Root Cause Analysis:
The cross-sectional image shows that an overcurrent passed through the ferrite bead, burning the internal winding and creating a blackened void. This failure was caused by excessive current. The manufacturer indicated that replacing the bead with one rated for a higher current capacity would resolve the issue. The component specification selected by the designer needs to be revised accordingly.

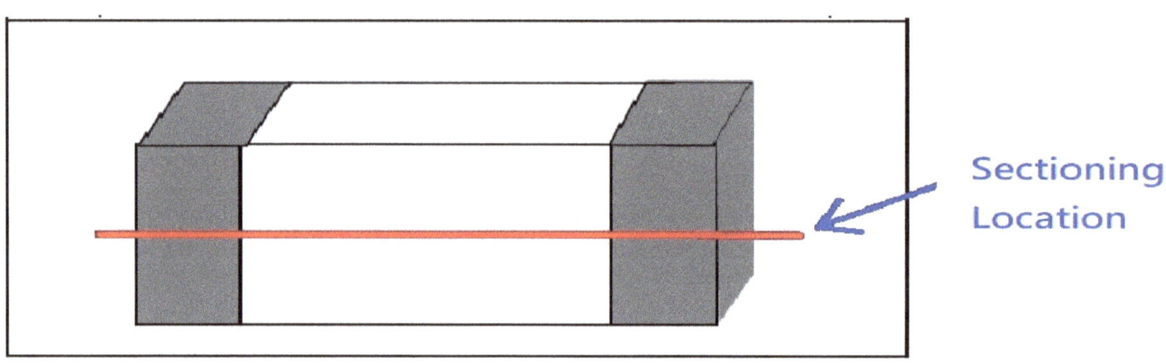

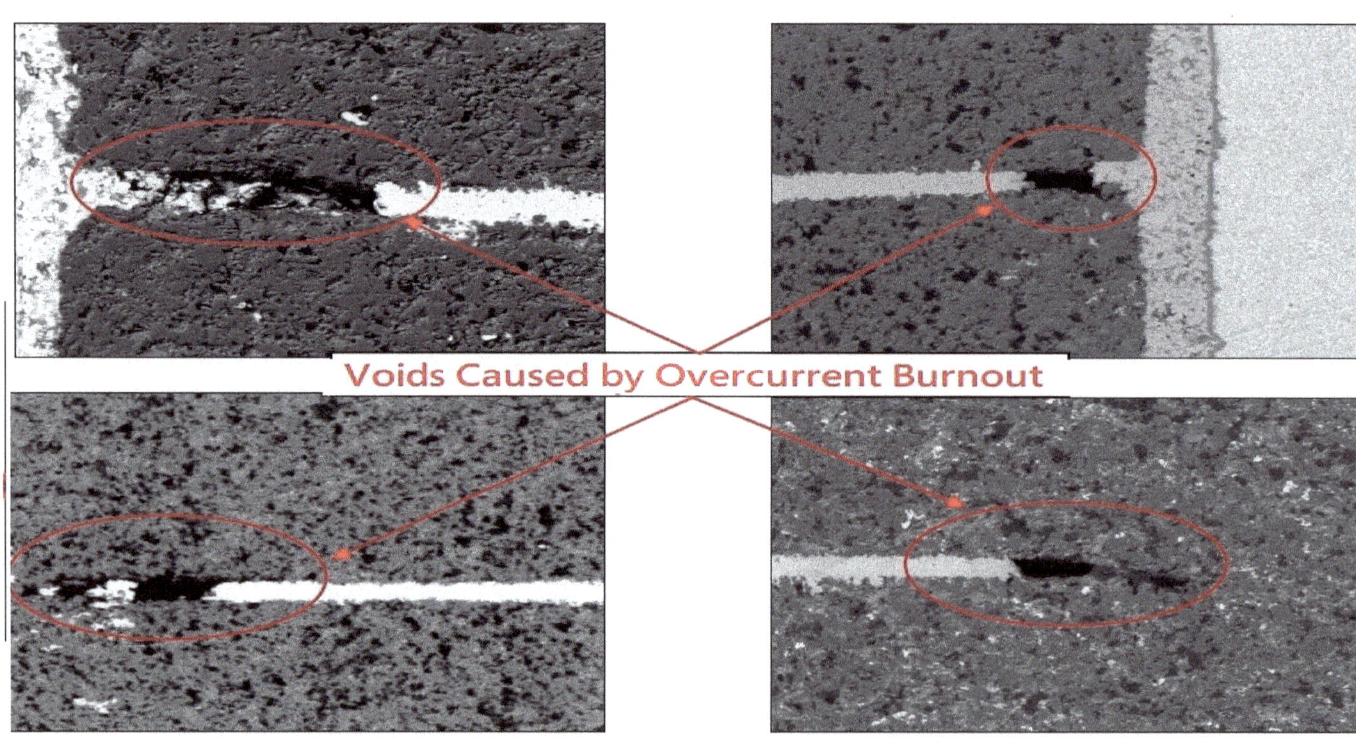

Figure 8-21. Cross-Section Image of Defective Ferrite Bead

Chapter 9:   More Miscellaneous Diseases

New engineers often make many mistakes, but what's even more surprising is that engineers tend to repeat the same mistakes over time. Typically, operators and production staff may not recognize design flaws, while designers may overlook manufacturing issues. Therefore, it is essential to promote cross-department communication and hold failure experience review meetings.

Quality is designed, not inspected. In fact, 80% of quality issues are determined during the design phase. This chapter presents examples of commonly made mistakes—let's explore and learn from them together!

PCB through-hole design error

The red arrow in Figure 9-1 indicates poor soldering of the IC pin. This is caused by the through-hole being too close to the IC pad. After heating, the solder leaks out of the through-hole, resulting in insufficient solder and a cold soldering. The PCB Layout engineer is responsible. This problem can be solved by simply moving the through-hole away. This type of design involving drilling holes in the pad often occurs, especially for novice designers.

Figure 9-2 shows two design errors in the QFN pad. One is the aforementioned through-hole in the pad, which causes solder loss and cold soldering. The other is the incorrect through-hole design on the heat sink. The large area of solder lifts the IC, causing one side of the IC to warp and become uneven, leading to poor soldering. Figure 9-3 shows the improved through-hole design. X-ray observation of the solder distribution shows good solder distribution.

Figure 9-1. PCB through-hole position design error

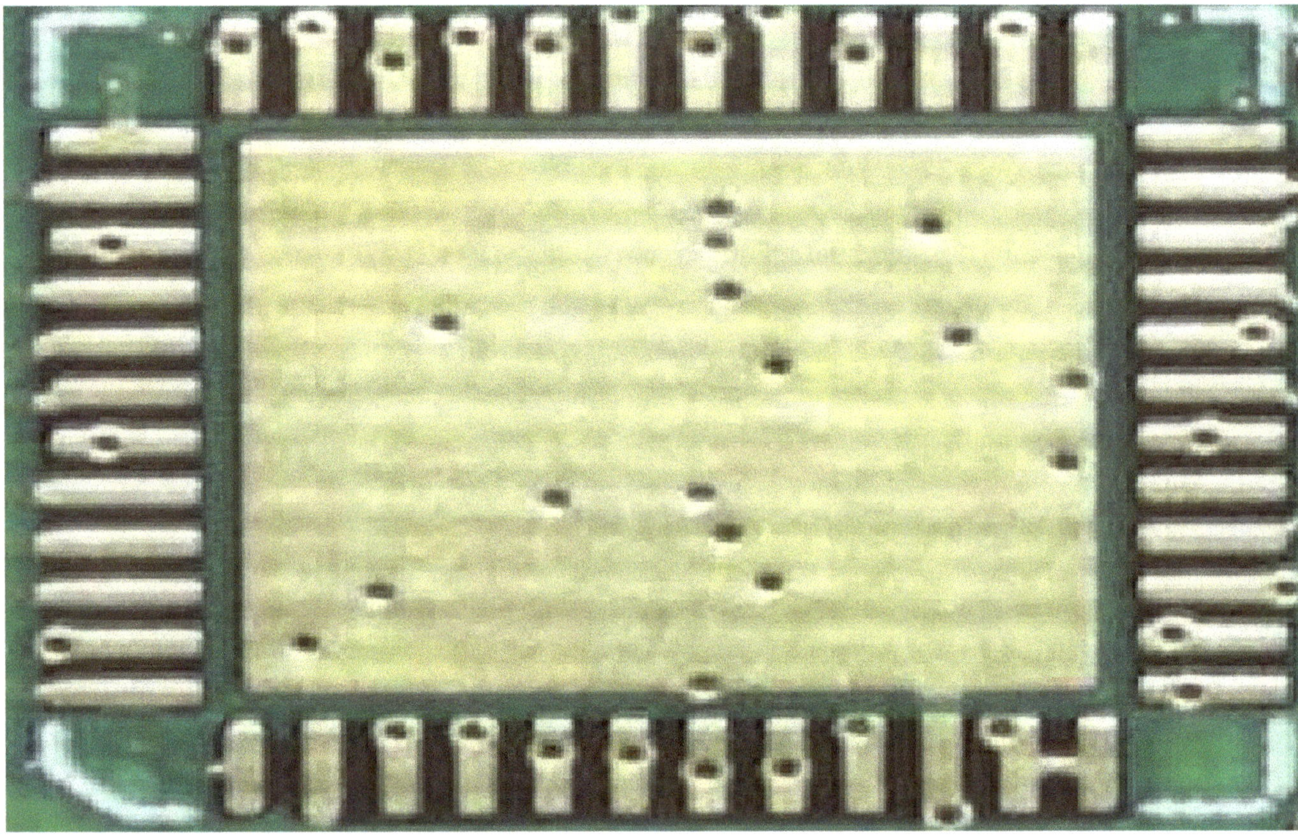

Figure 9-2. Example of incorrect PCB through-hole placement

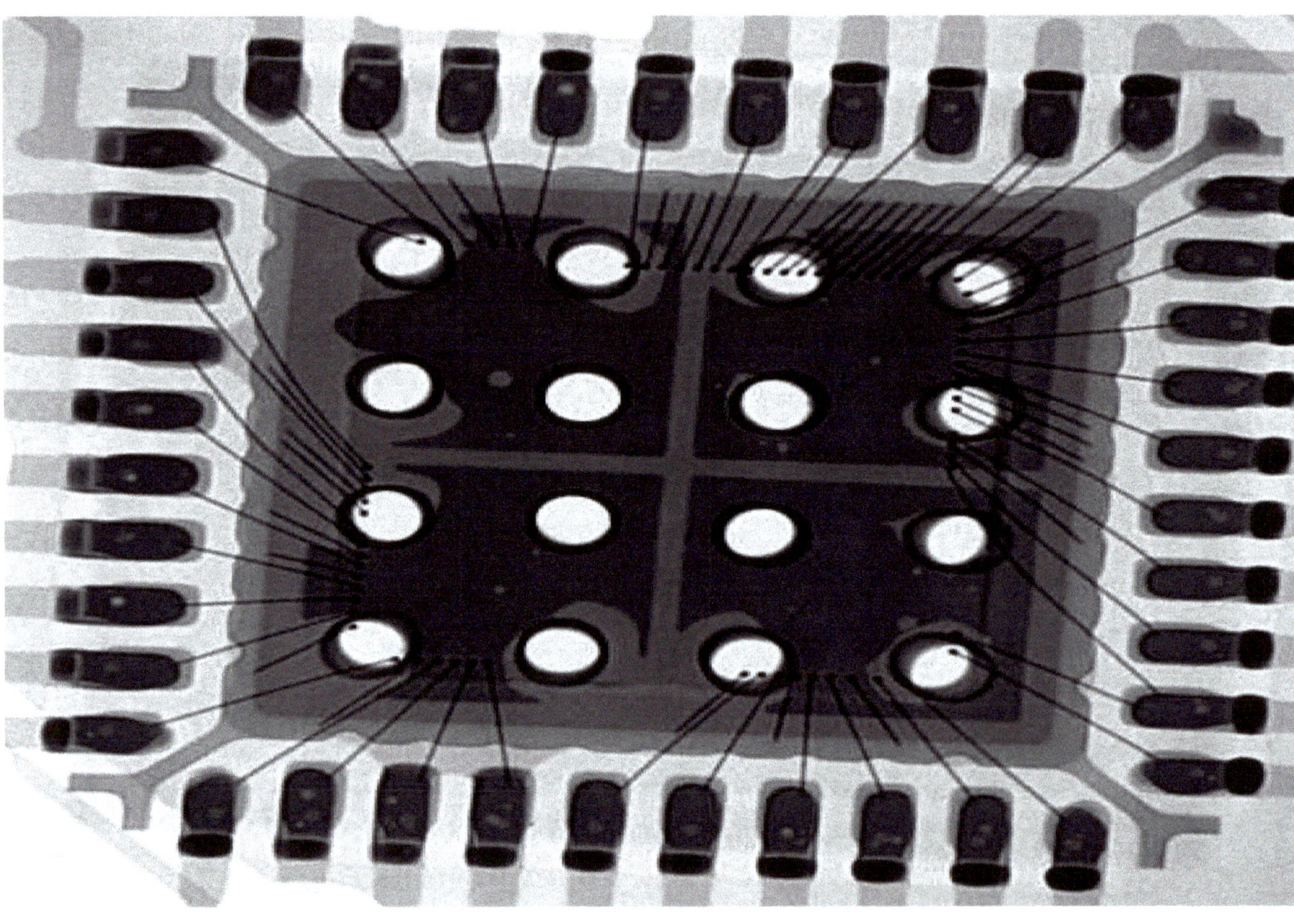

Figure 9-3. Improved QFN heat sink pad through-hole design

PCB Pad through-holes not filled

Figure 9-4 shows an example of an incorrect BGA IC pad design. BGA ICs have hundreds of solder balls and are typically designed using PCBs with 4 to 8 layers or more.
For example, Figure 9-4 shows 196 pads. As you can imagine, there isn't enough space for hundreds of layout traces. Furthermore, the gaps between pads are insufficient, and drilling holes in these gaps can easily cause short circuits. To route traces to inner layers, the idea is to drill holes directly through the pads.

The problem arises when a via is located directly on a pad. Solder paste is printed over the via, which still contains air inside. After reflow soldering at high temperatures, two types of issues may occur:

1. Solder Drainage**:** The solder paste flows into the via due to capillary action, resulting in insufficient solder on the pad and causing a cold soldering.
2. Trapped Air Expansion**:** If the via is not drilled through to the bottom layer of the PCB**,** the trapped air rapidly expands during heating. This pressure can form a bubble inside the solder joint**,** as shown in Figure 9-5.

A single solder ball is only about 0.5 mm in diameter, as small as a ballpoint pen tip. If more than 25% of the solder ball's volume is voided, the mechanical strength and reliability of the joint are significantly compromised. This issue is particularly critical in fine-pitch BGA or CSP packaging, where solder volume and integrity are crucial.

The improvement method for vias is shown in the right side of Figure 9-4. In this approach, the via is filled with conductive paste or resin (resin being the more cost-effective option) to eliminate trapped air**.** The surface is then plated over and polished to create a smooth, solderable finish. This prevents solder from draining into the via and improves joint reliability.

Other alternative techniques include laser-drilled microvias and blind/buried via technology, where very small vias are drilled between pads or internal layers to route traces without placing vias directly on pads. However, these methods significantly increase PCB manufacturing costs and are typically used in high-end or premium products.

Figure 9-4. PCB Design Error – Unfilled Via on Pad

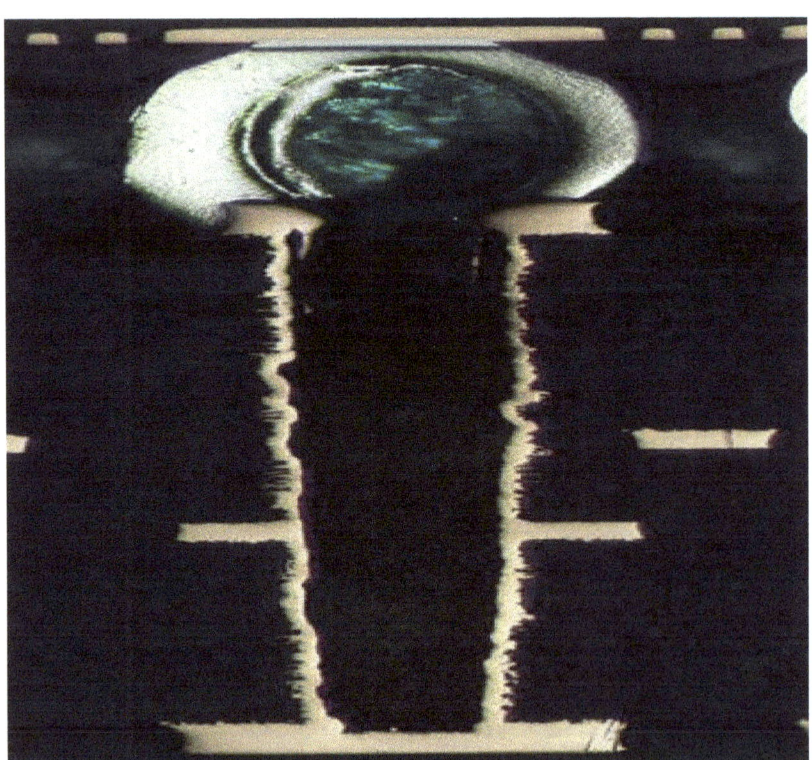

Figure 9-5. Unfilled PCB Via – Central Air Expansion Forms a Void After Heating

PCB manufacturing errors

Figure 9-6 shows a magnified microscope image of a non-conductive through-hole section. The cause of failure is a fracture in the copper foil wall at the red circle. A through-hole is cylindrical, and a completely non-conductive through-hole must have a circular fracture. A cross-sectional image will inevitably show fractures on both sides, usually symmetrically. Figure 9-6 clearly shows fractures on both sides. While it may temporarily conduct during electrical testing and pass inspection, the quality is extremely unstable.

Cause Analysis: Upon examining the fracture area, a gap was observed between the central filled resin and the copper layer. In areas without fractures, the resin and copper were well bonded. It is determined that during the resin via filling process, moisture or air may have remained on the via walls. When the board underwent high-temperature processing, the expansion created outward pressure, causing the copper layer to crack. However, since part of the copper surface remained in contact, the issue could not be detected during electrical testing. The fracture occurred later when exposed to high temperatures at the customer's reflow process.

Suggested Improvement Measures:
Increase the copper layer thickness — raise the plating thickness of the via hole from 300μ" to over 600μ" to enhance the copper layer's resistance to stress. Revise the resin dehumidification and baking process: change the original condition of 150°C for one hour to a stepped baking process — first bake at 50°C for one hour, then at 110°C for one hour, and finally at 150°C for one hour. This low-temperature pre-bake helps to drive out moisture and air before curing the resin, thereby preventing moisture or air from remaining on the via walls.

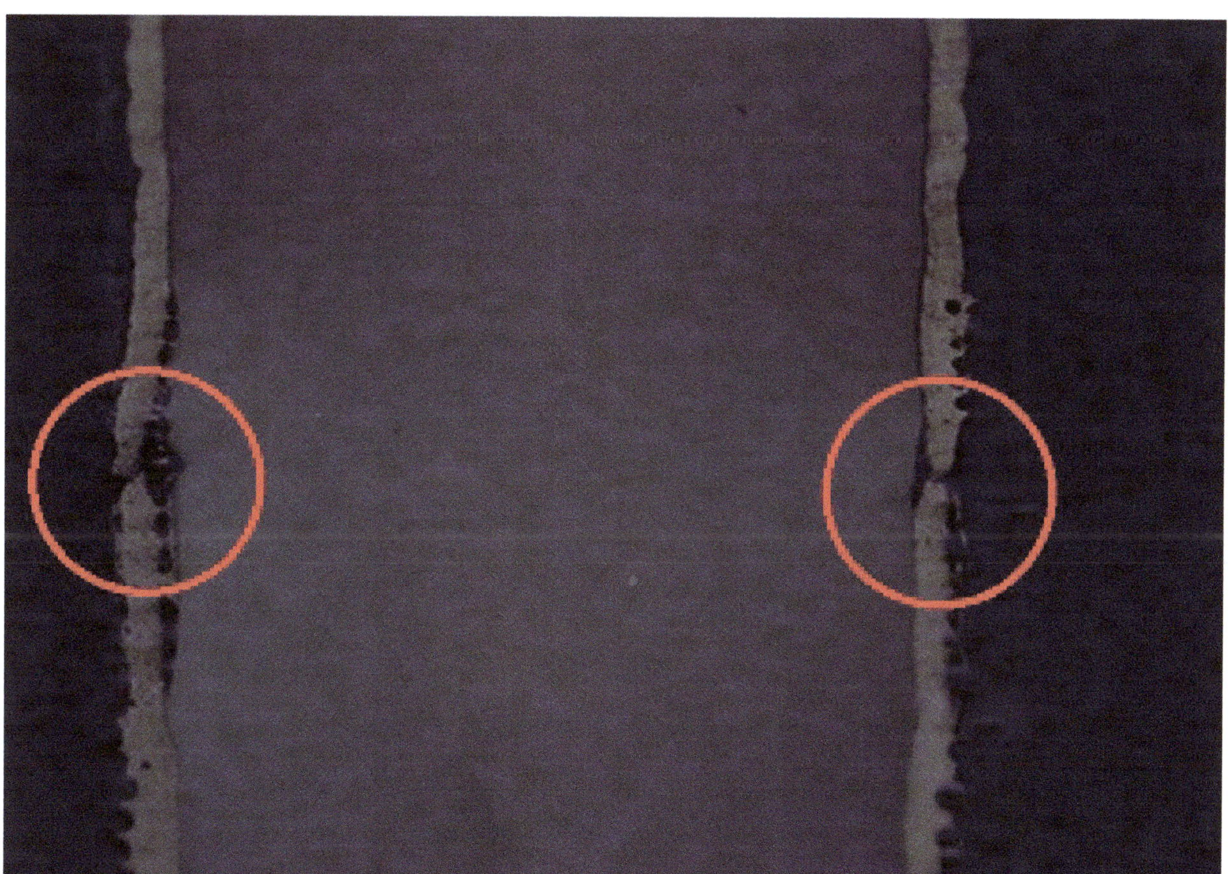

Figure 9-6. PCB through-hole fracture cross-section

Figure 9-7 shows that when the through hole was filled with green resin, it overflowed the through hole and covered the pad, causing the solder ball to be unable to solder to the pad. This defect was discovered by the sectioning method.

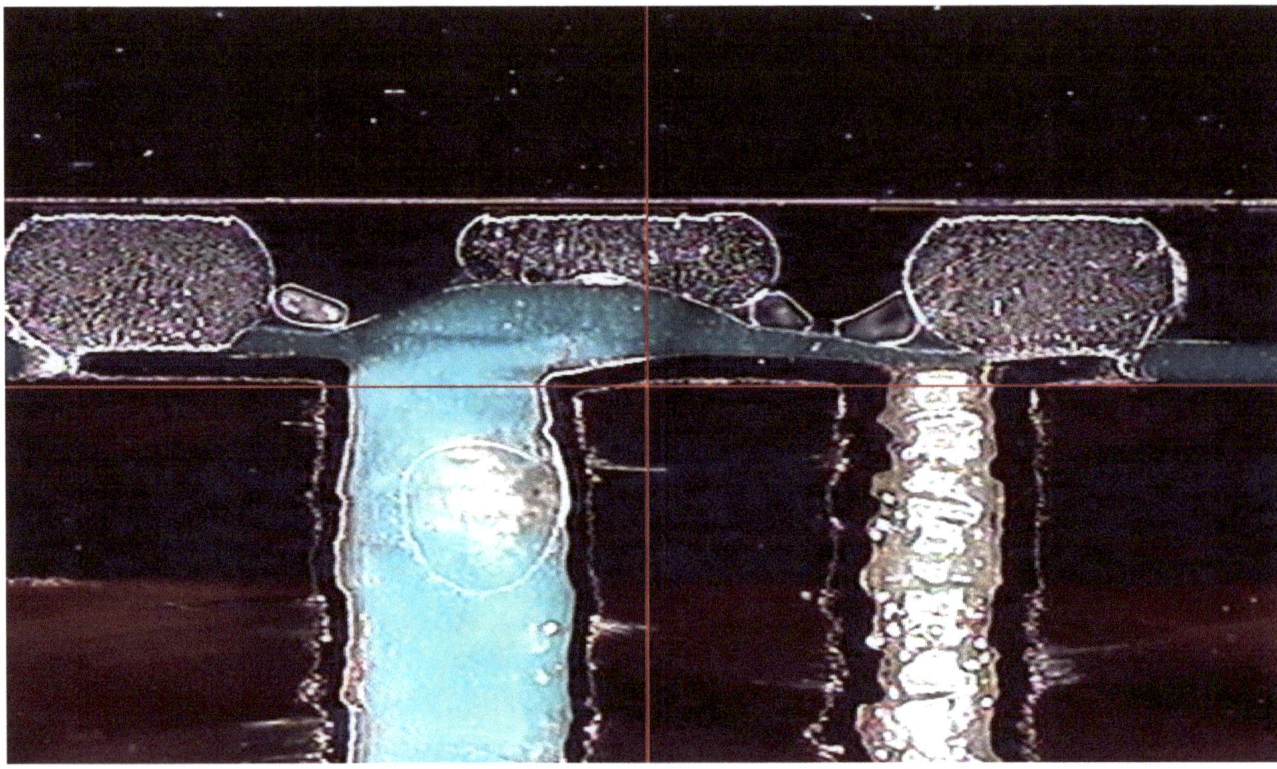

Figure 9-7. Overflow of Green Resin from Via Fill

Figure 9-8 shows pad oxidation. In the red-circled area, the BGA pad copper foil has oxidized, turning a dull dark red color, which causes solderability issues. This was detected during IQC incoming inspection and material feeding on the production line. The PCB supplier was requested to retrieve the boards for reprocessing.

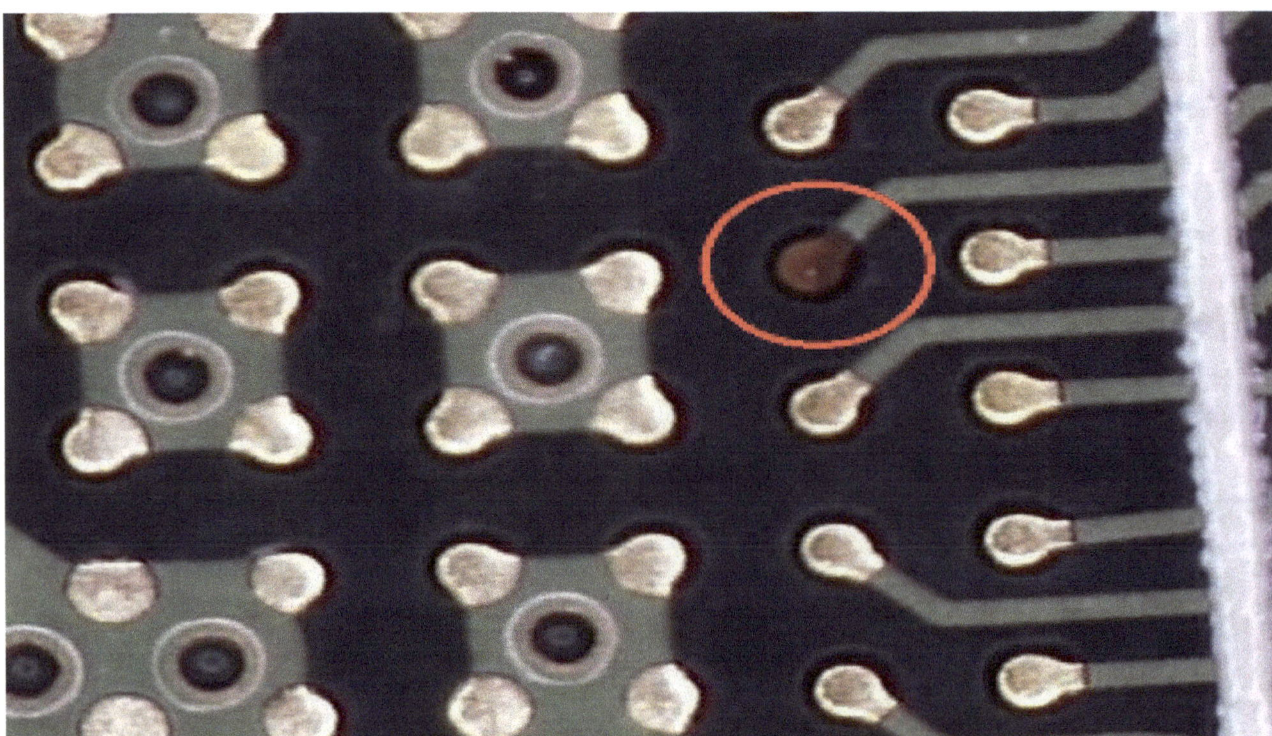

Figure 9-8. PAD Oxidation

Mouse Sensor Pollution

An optical mouse has a red light-emitting diode (LED) underneath. The light generated by the LED passes through a prism lens and illuminates the surface of the surface. A sensor receives the signal and reads the image of the surface through the lens. Comparing the images thousands of times per second, it determines the direction of mouse movement. Contamination on the sensor can cause errors in image reading and incorrect mouse movement.

Figure 9-9: The left image shows a magnified view of the mouse sensor's reading window. The right image shows a black foreign particle that has entered the sensing area, causing malfunction. A dust-proof sticker is applied to the sensor surface at the factory. During processing or rework, a protective solder mask tape should be applied to prevent dust, debris, or flux from contaminating the sensor surface. The work environment must be kept clean, and the protective sticker should only be removed after processing is complete. Ensure the sensor window faces downward to minimize the chance of dust intrusion.

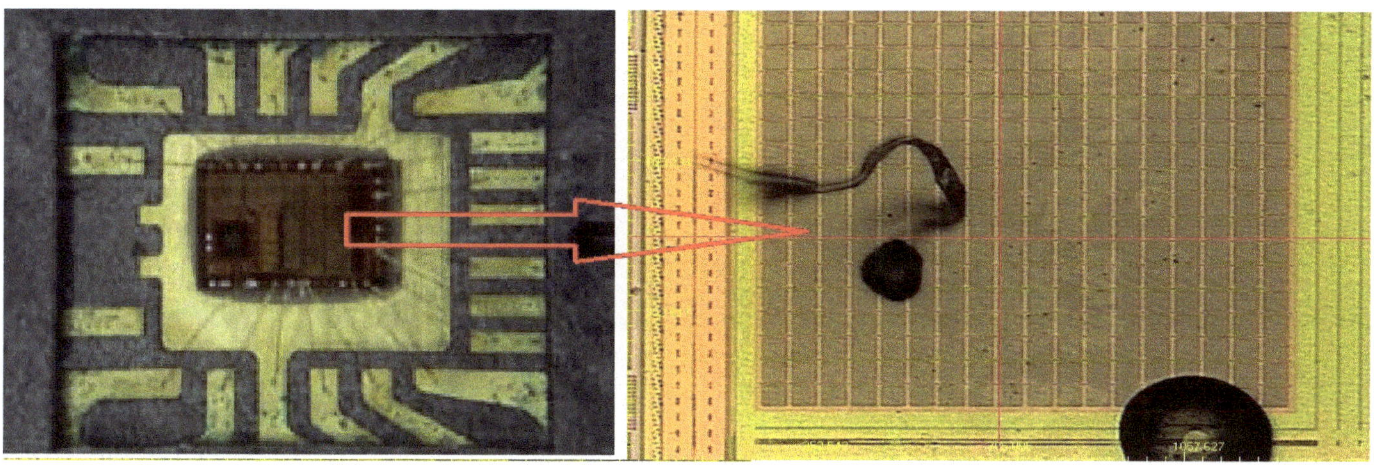

圖 9-9. 滑鼠 Sensor 讀取窗放大圖

IC gold wire breakage

There are many reasons for IC wire breakage, including excessive pressure from the needle during bonding, which can cause deformation of the gold ball; wire thinning; insufficient pressure from the needle, which can lead to a loose bond between the solder joint and the chip; and other factors, such as excessive processing temperature, stress fracture, and high current melting. X-ray and decap analysis can be used for fault analysis. Figures 9-10 show X-ray images of an IC, showing a wire break at the neck. The wire is melted, indicating current melting. Power surges, reverse voltage, and EOS electrostatic discharge (ESD) damage are all possible causes.

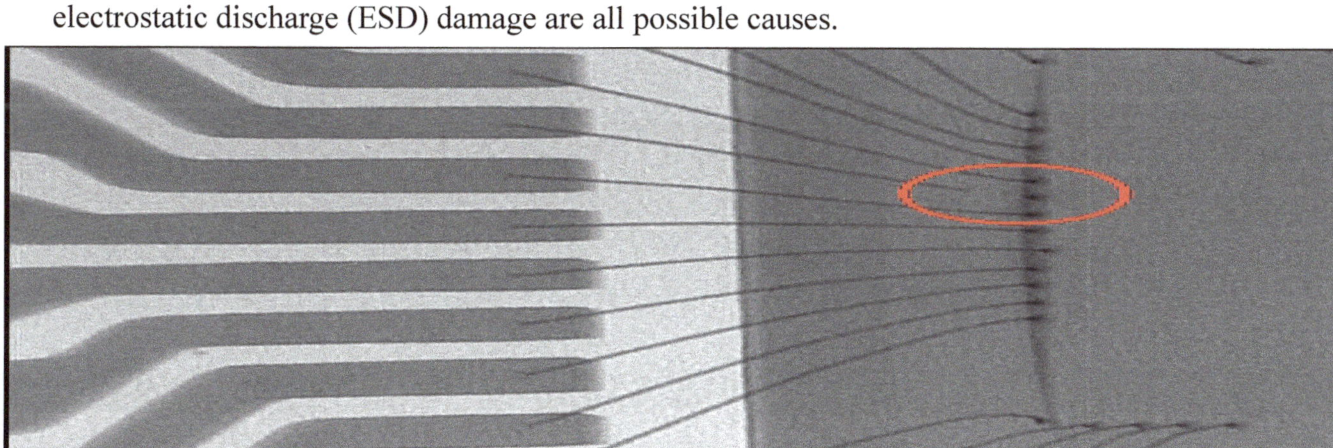

Figure 9-10. X-ray of a broken gold wire

Another case is shown in Figure 9-11, which is a de-cap image taken with an electron microscope. The image shows gold wire breakage caused by thermal expansion of the LED encapsulant, generating stress that pulled and broke both wires simultaneously. This issue is related to the thermal expansion coefficient of the LED packaging material.

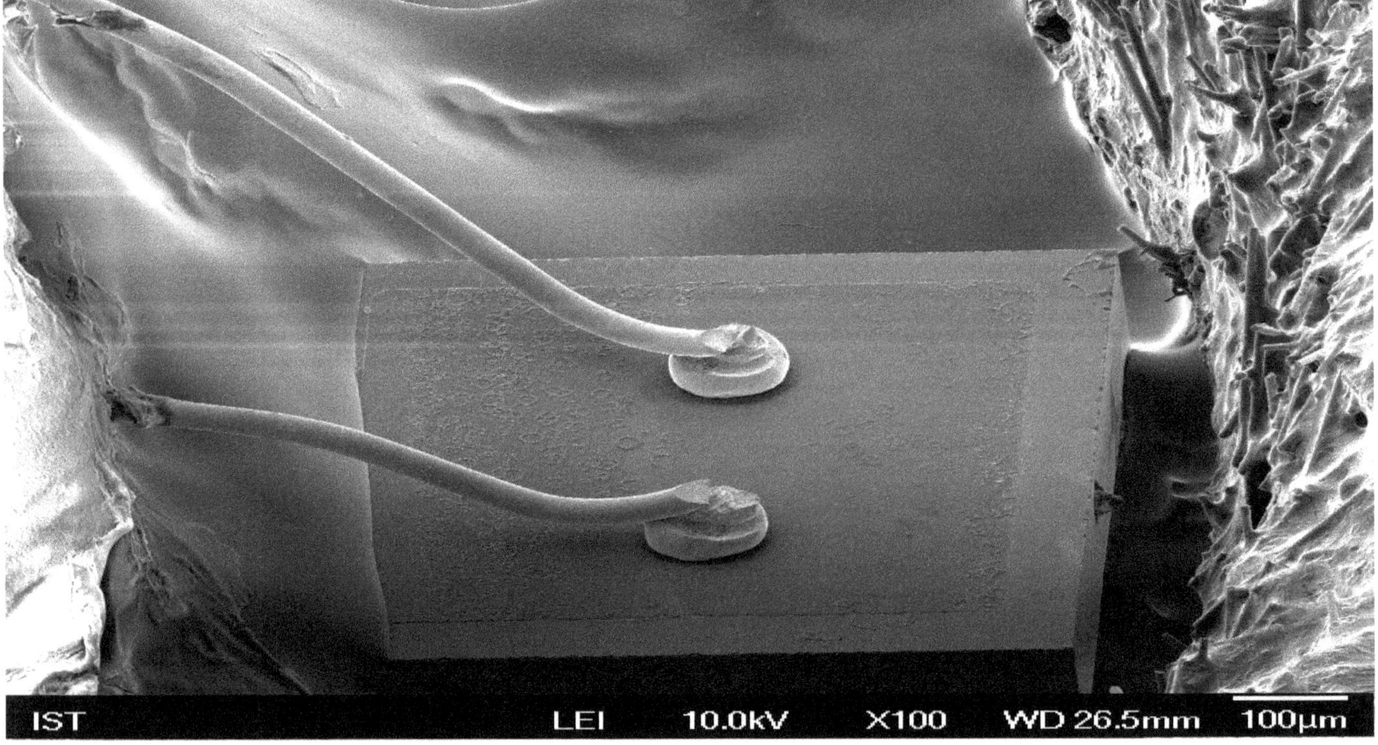

Figure 9-11. Gold Wire De-cap Image 1

The image below shows misaligned wire bonding, where the second bonding process damages the first bond, causing wire breakage defects.

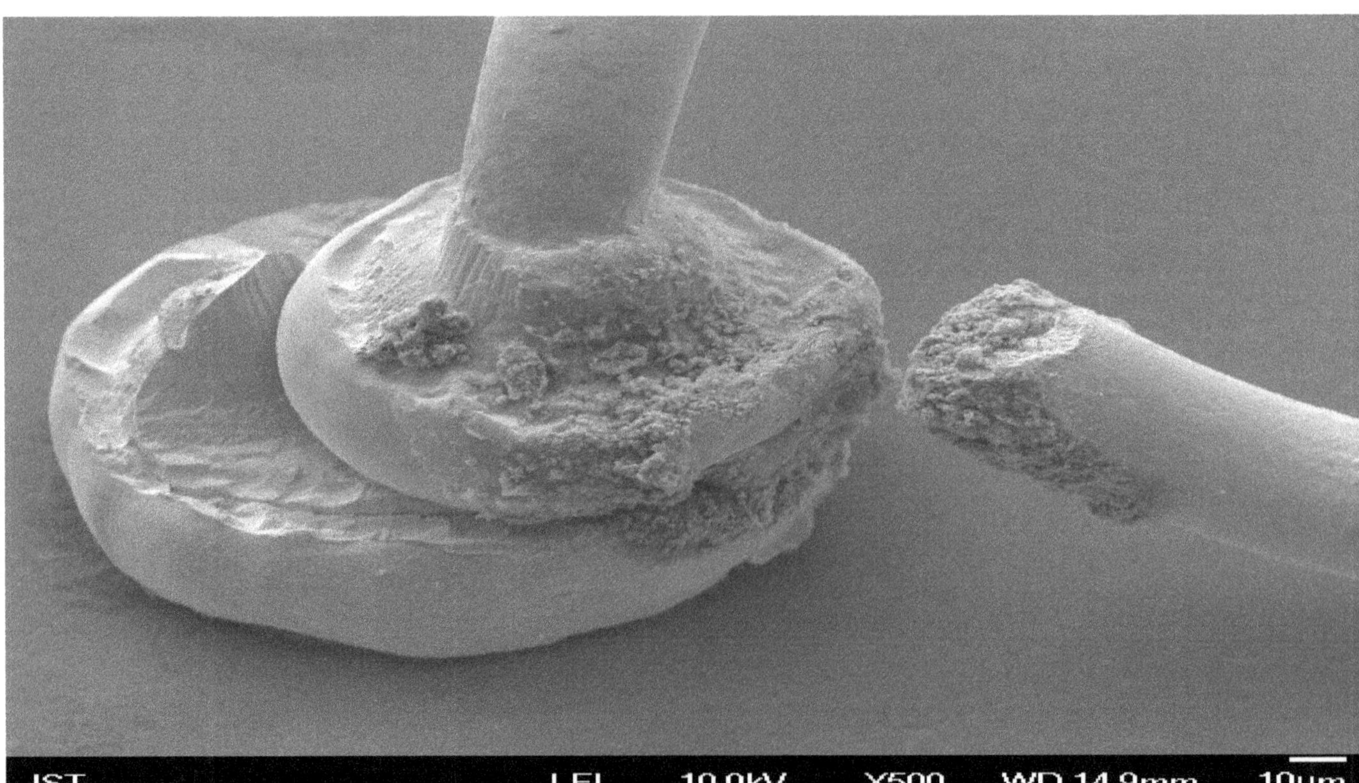

Figure 9-12. Gold Wire De-cap Image 2

SMT Processing Problems

Figure 9-13 shows an electrical short circuit caused by a solder bridge. The electrical function can be used to detect the defect.

Figure 9-13. Solder bridge short circuit

Figure 9-14 shows a stress fracture on the top of a capacitor. When removing the component with a soldering iron, it was found to have automatically split in two. This most commonly occurs on the edge of the board.

If the same component fails in random locations on the board, it's usually due to component quality issues. If all failures occur in the same location, it's usually due to a processing issue, such as stress from manual board separation.

Figure 9-14. Capacitor stress cracking

Defective button battery

The nominal voltage specification for the button-type lithium battery is 3.2V. During incoming inspection in China, defective units with low voltages ranging from 2.7V to 2.8V were found.

Figure 9-15 shows the disassembled view of the button battery. The root cause analysis concluded that, during the manufacturing process, the internal separator film was unevenly coated. The color changed from white to yellow, resulting in uneven current discharge in some batteries. This led to a failure to meet standard performance requirements, causing the low voltage issue.

Figure 9-15. Disassembled View of Button Cell

Heidelberg and Mount Titlis scenery

Quartz oscillator crystal defective

Quartz Crystal Oscillator (XTAL) is an electronic component that generates a high-precision oscillation frequency and functions like the "heart" of a product. Below are examples of XTAL-related quality incidents:

1. **Issue:** Oscillation frequency instability.
   Root Cause: Improper matching of negative resistance.
2. **Issue:** XTAL does not oscillate, resulting in product malfunction.
   Root Cause: Crystal chip fracture.
3. **Issue:** Frequency abnormality during temperature rise, leading to product malfunction.
   Root Cause: Misalignment in crystal cutting angle.
4. **Issue:** Frequency drift occurs when temperature exceeds 40°C.
   Root Cause: Scratches on the crystal chip.
5. **Issue:** Frequency deviation or no oscillation, resulting in product malfunction.
   Root Cause: Foreign matter on the crystal chip.
6. **Issue:** Frequency instability around 40–60°C.
   Root Cause: Inadequate curing of silver conductive adhesive.
7. **Issue:** Frequency drift caused by physical impact, resulting in screen flickering on TVs.
   Root Cause: Poor silver adhesive quality.
8. **Issue:** No oscillation at elevated temperatures, causing product malfunction.
   Root Cause: External current-limiting resistor too large.
9. **Issue:** Short circuit.
   Root Cause: Poor tin plating on terminals; solder melt during reflow caused a short.
10. **Other Issue:** Insufficient hermetic sealing.

Additional Analysis:

- **Item 1 – Improper Matching of Negative Resistance:**
  This issue is primarily the responsibility of the circuit designer. The incorrect selection of matching capacitors can cause oscillation frequency deviation. If measurement equipment is unavailable, the designer can bring the finished product to the crystal supplier for negative resistance testing to determine the optimal capacitor values.
- **Item 2 – Crystal Chip Fracture:**
  This failure is typically attributed to production. Improper handling, impact, or dropping of the component can cause the crystal chip to crack. A common example is when operators hit the PCBA against a workbench to remove excess solder residue during rework. Since quartz crystals are fragile and glass-like, such handling practices must be avoided.
- **Item 8 – Excessive External Current-Limiting Resistor:**
  This is also a design issue. An overly large current-limiting resistor reduces the drive current, causing the XTAL to fail to start oscillating when the temperature rises, resulting in functional failure.

Figure 9-16 shows a fractured XTAL chip. The arrow on the left indicates the breakage point of the quartz crystal.

Figure 9-16. XTAL Chip Fracture

Figure 9-17 shows scratches on the quartz chip, which can easily lead to frequency drift.

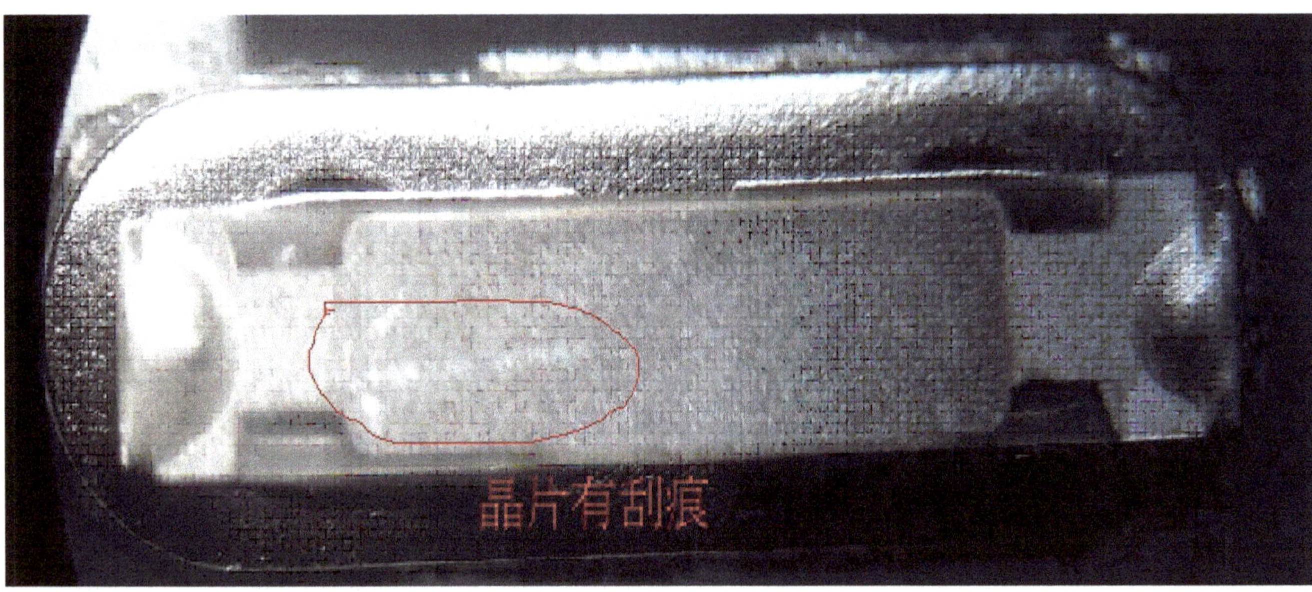

Figure 9-17. Scratch on Crystal Chip

Figure 9-18 reveals the presence of foreign matter on the crystal chip. EDX analysis indicates the contaminant is composed of 96% silver. The silver particles originated from delamination of the silver-plated electrode terminals. Any foreign substance, such as dust, attached to the crystal surface can affect frequency accuracy.

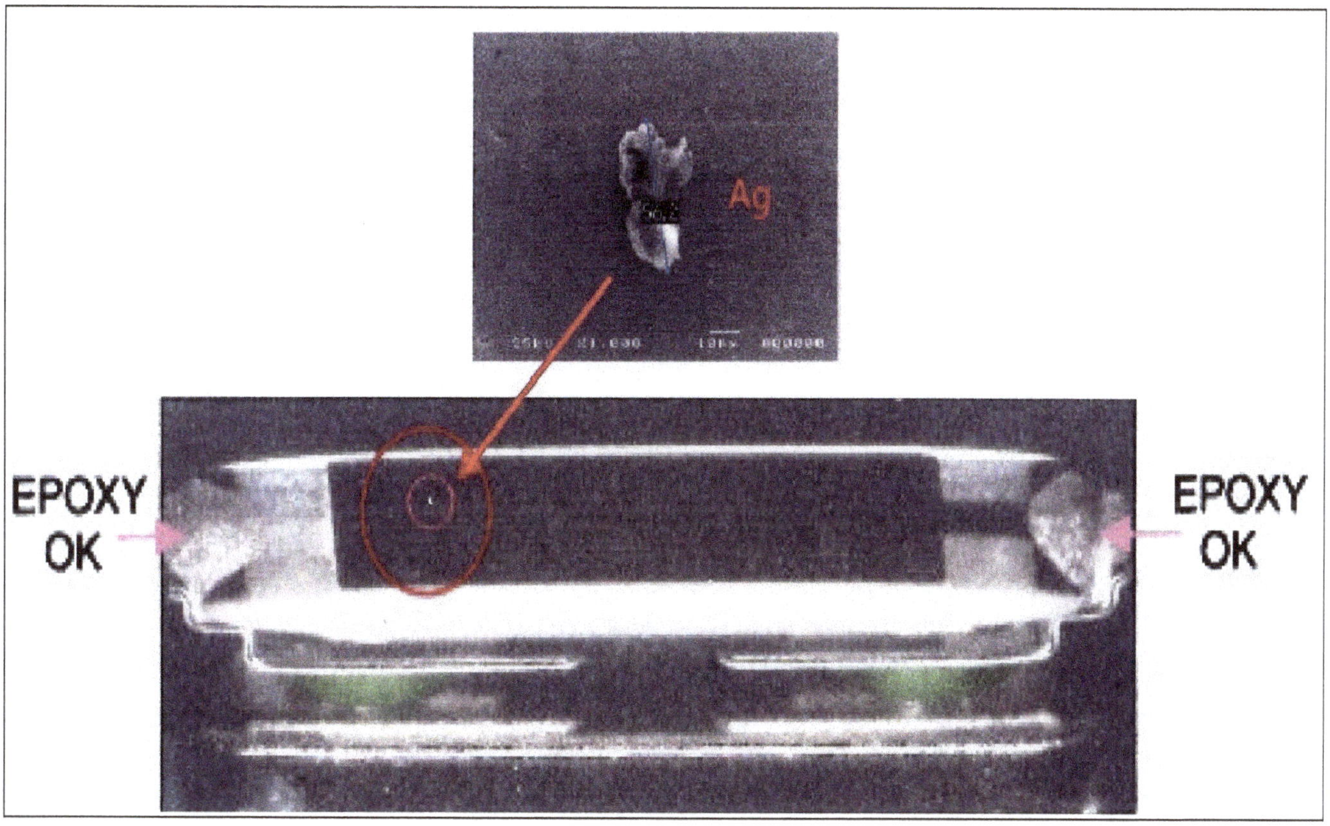

Figure 9-18. Foreign Material on Crystal Chip Identified as Silver (Ag) by EDX Analysis

Figure 9-19 shows excessive solder melt due to high-temperature reflow, caused by poor tin plating on the terminals. The bottom view of the terminal reveals a large area of silver-white solder overflow, resulting in a short circuit between adjacent terminals—clearly a plating defect.

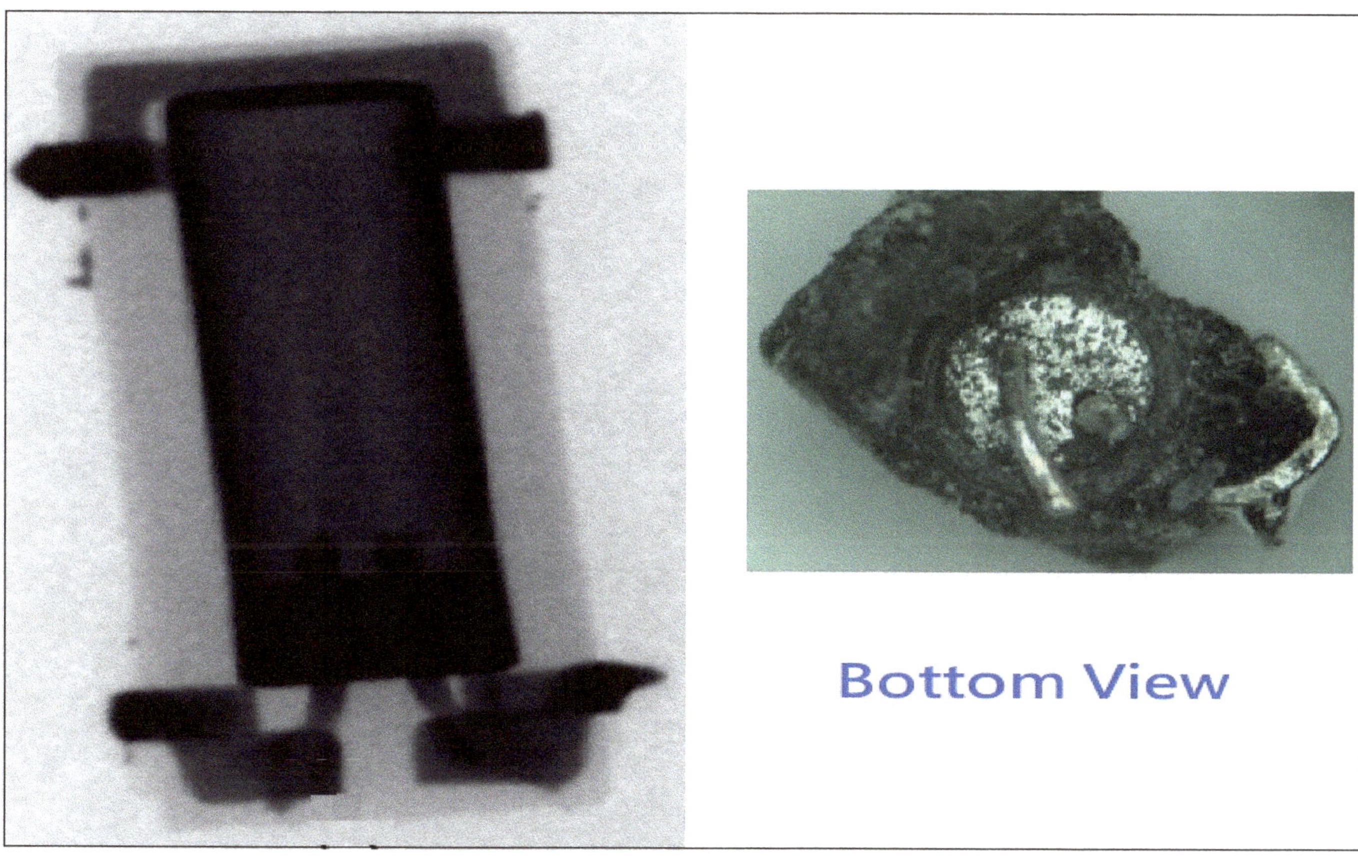

Figure 9-19. XTAL Terminal Short Circuit Detected via Multimeter Due to Heat-Induced Solder Flow on Terminal Plating

Printing ink pollution

Production dates are often printed on the PCB for lot traceability. In Figure 9-20, uncured ink leaked through a via hole (indicated by the red arrow) and flowed to the backside of the PCB. Unfortunately, the backside happened to be the keypad circuit area with carbon-printed traces for a remote control. Once the ink hardened, it caused poor key response.

Corrective Action: Use fast-drying ink specifically designed for this purpose and relocate the date code printing to an area without via holes.

Figure 9-20. Printing Ink Contamination

Auger Electron Spectroscopy (Auger): [Non-destructive analysis]

When incoming materials are suspected of contamination—such as PCB pad copper contamination with phosphorus (black pad phenomenon) or solderability issues due to oxidation—analysis using Auger Electron Spectroscopy (Auger) or Electron Spectroscopy for Chemical Analysis (ESCA) can be considered.

Auger is a surface-sensitive analytical tool capable of detecting elemental composition and chemical bonding states within the top 5–7 nm of a material. It provides micro-layer surface analysis, allowing layer-by-layer identification of surface and interfacial contaminants. For example, if the surface of a PCB solder pad shows an excessively high phosphorus content (over 10%), it may result in poor solderability due to the formation of a nickel black pad layer.

PCB Cost Reduction Options (OSP Technology)

Electroless Nickel/Gold (ENIG) PCB pads often encounter issues such as incomplete etchant cleaning, abnormal cleaning agent concentration, phosphorus contamination, and poor plating quality. These problems can cause PCB oxidation, black pad formation, and solderability failures. Due to these quality concerns, many major manufacturers prohibit the reuse of ENIG PCB pads. My Japanese customer specifically requested switching from ENIG to OSP (Organic Solderability Preservatives).

OSP technology chemically forms a thin protective film on bare copper surfaces, providing oxidation resistance, thermal shock resistance, and moisture resistance. Although OSP boards do not have as long a shelf life or durability as ENIG boards, proper handling—such as preventing oxidation during incoming inspection and vacuum packaging to avoid moisture—ensures that OSP boards deliver better solder joint strength and reliability compared to ENIG, while also offering lower material costs.
However, OSP is not suitable for applications requiring long-term oxidation protection in harsh environments, such as gold finger contacts on memory cards.

Oblique viewing microscope

Electron Microscope for Lateral Observation of Solder Joints

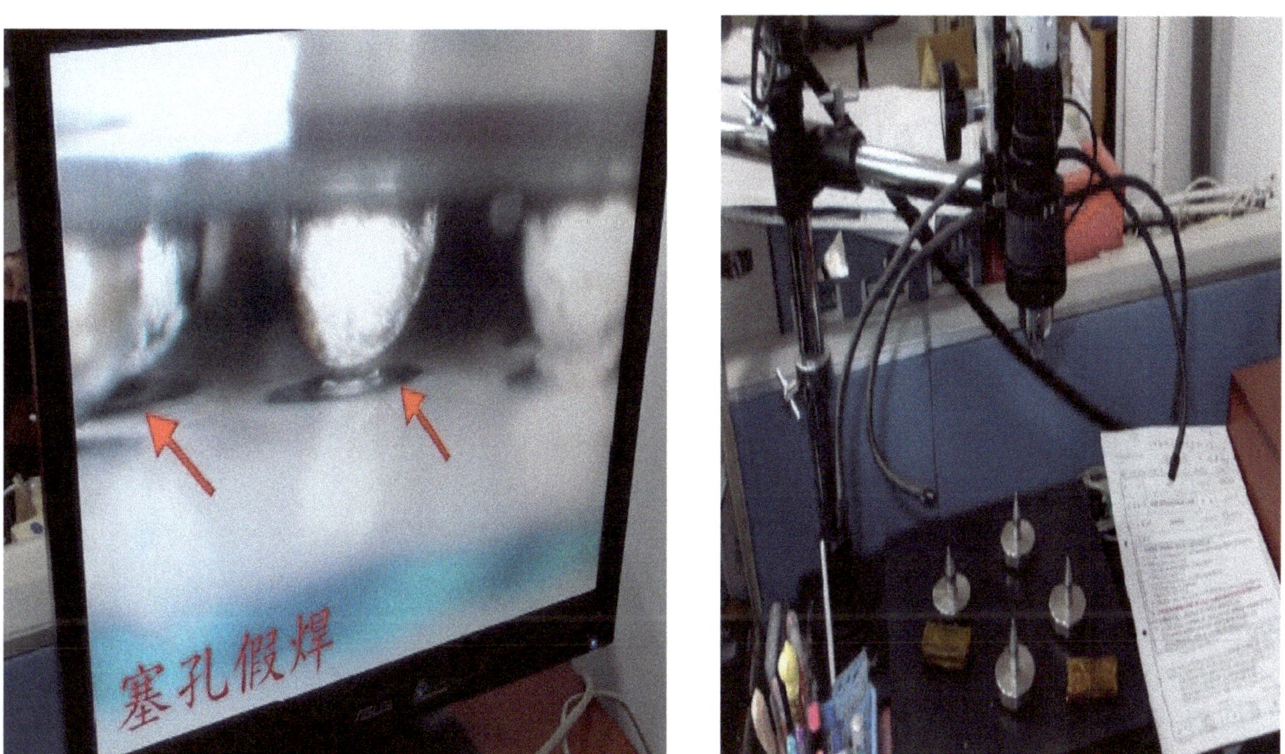

Figure 9-21. Side View Showing BGA Solder Ball Joint Condition

Variable Resistor Failure Analysis

Variable resistor resistance curves can be categorized into several types, each tailored to specific application requirements.

1. Linear Taper: The resistance changes linearly with rotation angle or sliding distance. This is commonly used in applications requiring uniform adjustment, such as speed control and voltage control. (Type B)
2. Logarithmic Taper: The resistance changes logarithmically with rotation angle or sliding distance. This is commonly used in audio applications, as the human ear perceives sound logarithmically. (Type A)
3. Reverse Logarithmic Taper: The resistance changes antilogarithmically with rotation angle or sliding distance. This is commonly used in certain applications requiring adjustment using a different logarithmic pattern. (Type C)
4. S-curve Taper: The resistance changes slowly in the middle and more rapidly at the ends, forming an S-shaped curve. This is commonly used in specialized control applications, such as light dimming.

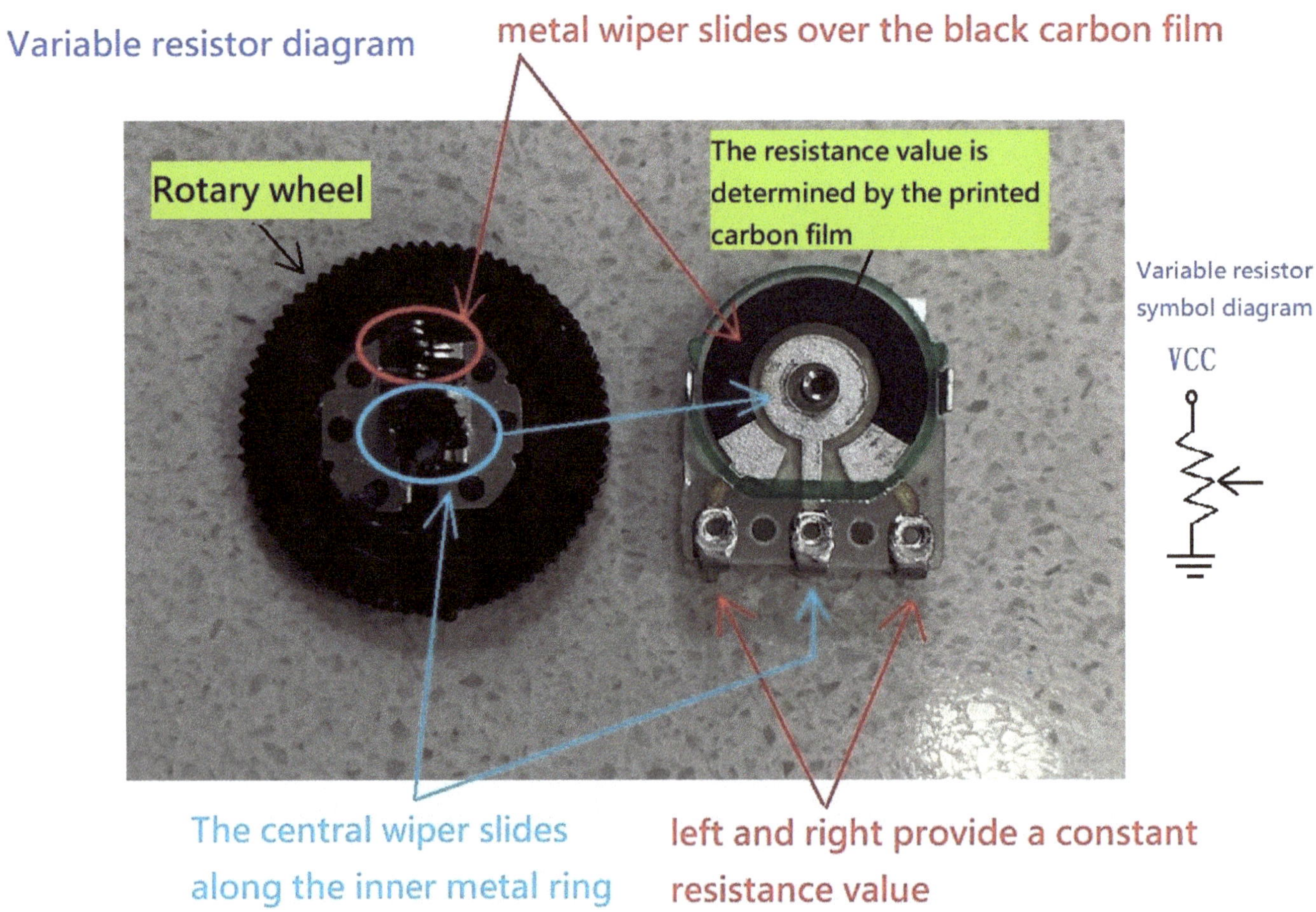

Figure 9-22. Basic Schematic Diagram of a Variable Resistor

The most common failure points of variable resistors are the contact plates and carbon film. Failures are typically caused by the following:

1. Wear: Prolonged use causes friction between the contact plates and the carbon film resistor element, eventually leading to wear and poor contact.
2. Oxidation: When exposed to air, the metal contact plates oxidize and sulfide, forming an

insulating layer that affects conductivity.

3. Dirt and Dust: Dust and other contaminants enter the varistor, affecting the conductivity and sliding properties of the contact plates.
4. Corrosion: Humid environments or chemicals can cause corrosion of metal components, further affecting the performance of the contact plates.
5. Improper Contact Pressure: Insufficient pressure between the contact plates and the carbon film resistor can result from elastic fatigue over time or design issues. This can lead to poor contact. Excessive contact pressure can quickly cause scratches and powdering on the carbon film.
6. Mechanical Damage: External impact or improper handling during use can cause deformation or damage to the contact plates.

You often hear a noise when turning a knob on your audio system, also known as sliding noise. This noise in variable resistors is usually caused by poor contact or aging. This noise is often heard when adjusting the resistance value. Here are some possible solutions:

1. Clean the contacts: Use an appropriate cleaner (such as contact cleaner) to clean the resistor's contacts to remove dirt and oxides.
2. Check the contact pressure: Ensure sufficient sliding contact pressure to ensure good electrical contact.
3. Replace the resistor: If the resistor is aged or damaged, replace it with a new variable resistor.
4. Choose a high-quality resistor: Choose a brand-name, high-quality variable resistor, such as ALPS, with phosphor bronze or alloy contact plates, nickel or silver plating, anti-sulfurization treatment, and carbon film chemistry. These generally provide better contact quality and a longer lifespan.

If the problem persists, you may need to further review your circuit design or consider using a different component type, such as a digital potentiometer.

There are a few things to keep in mind when designing and using a variable resistor. First, avoid using it in a humid environment. Second, the variable resistor is used to set a voltage and should not pass excessive current.

Failure Case Analysis: Electric Blanket Emitting Smoke and Causing Fire

Customers have reported serious incidents of electric blankets emitting smoke and catching fire, primarily due to quality issues with the variable resistor. The variable resistor has three fixed terminals, which are metal hinged to the PCB. If the hinge becomes loose or cracks due to overvoltage, it can cause poor contact.

Electric blankets use variable resistors to control temperature. The higher the voltage at the center terminal, the higher the temperature. Because the grounded terminal's hinge is loose, it creates a short circuit, creating a series resistor from VCC to the center terminal. This means the center terminal voltage equals VCC, permanently commanding the electric blanket to heat at maximum power. This can lead to overheating, smoke, and even fire.

As shown in Figure 9-23, the improvement focuses on the shape of the terminal clinch. In the original design, the clinch area featured a cut slot, which weakened its structural integrity. The revised design adopts an integrated circular form, which offers the strongest holding force. After clinching, as shown in the right side of Figure 9-22, the entire ring is uniformly compressed. Some manufacturers even use a punch to add extra press points on the ring for reinforcement.

It is important to note that the variable resistor will undergo the customer's reflow soldering process, where repeated thermal expansion and contraction pose a durability challenge.
Using an electronic punch press for the clinching operation helps ensure consistent force, avoiding issues such as insufficient pressure or excessive force that could damage the PCB.

From a circuit design perspective, it is recommended to add a pull-down or pull-up resistor to the center terminal of the variable resistor. This ensures that in the event of contact failure, the terminal voltage is pulled to a defined and safe level, rather than left floating in an indeterminate state.

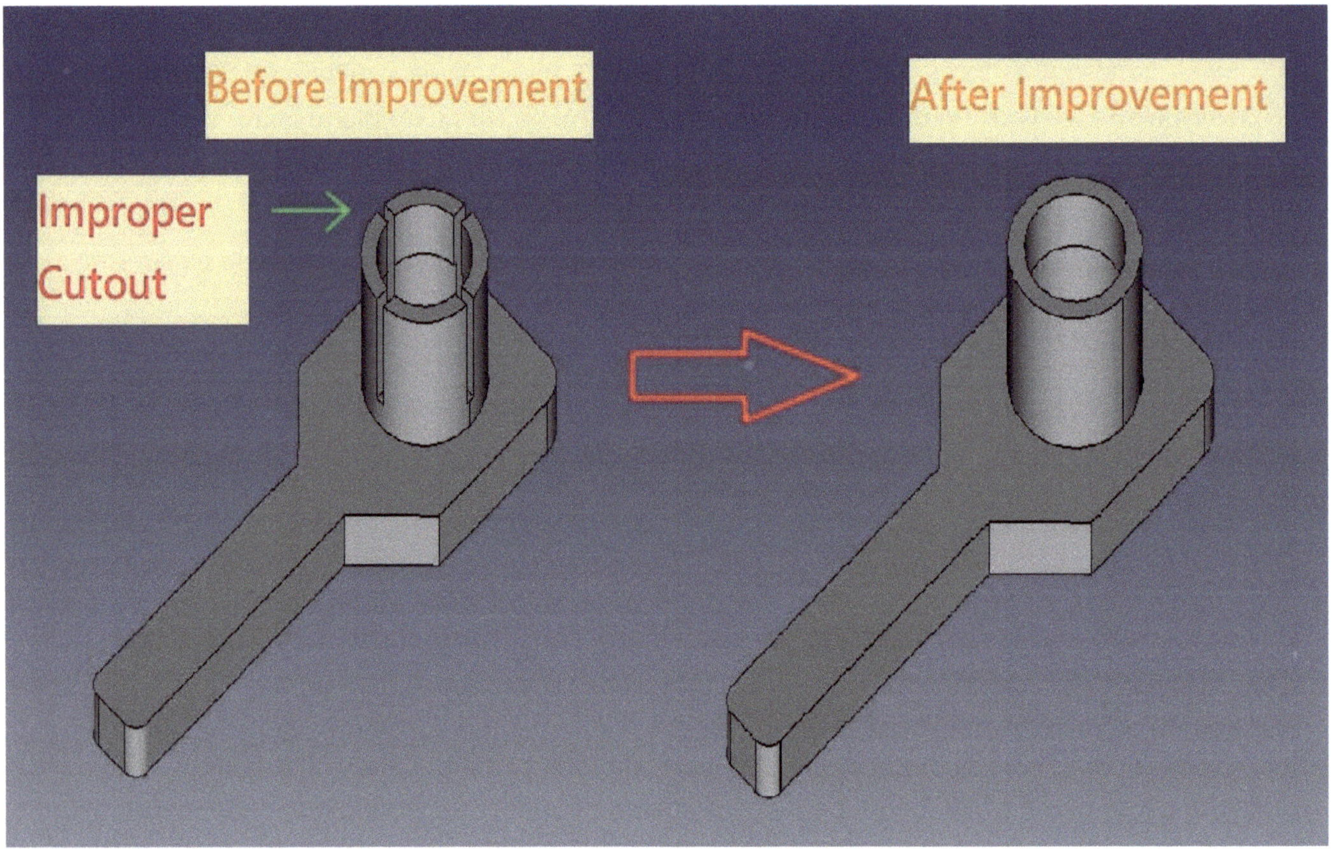

Figure 9-23. Appearance of Variable Resistor Terminals Before and After Clinching

Conclusion:

Factory quality control activities include: ISO 9000 (International Quality Management System Standard), ISO 14000 (Environmental Management), ISO 13485 (Medical Devices), SA8000 (Social Accountability Standard), TS16949 (Automotive Industry), RoHS, WEEE (Waste Electrical and Electronic Equipment Directive), REACH, Six Sigma (6σ), SPC (Statistical Process Control), Process Capability Index (Cpk), QCTC, PPAP (Production Part Approval Process), APQP (Advanced Product Quality Planning), FMEA (Failure Mode and Effects Analysis), GRR (Gage Repeatability and Reproducibility), Product Life Cycle, Greenhouse Gases, Carbon Footprint, Carbon Credits, 6S, etc. Implementing all of these can be quite complex and challenging, testing everyone's ability to execute thoroughly.

This book is based on practical experience. While it may not delve deeply into every possible root cause of defects, we hope that the useful parts can offer value and learning. If there are any inaccuracies or misjudgments in perspective, we sincerely welcome your understanding and feedback. It is a humble sharing of some hard-earned experience, and we wish everyone great success and a soaring future in the thriving electronics industry.

Attached are photos taken during business trips and travels—such beautiful scenery! Wishing you smooth work and a victorious return.

Arc de Triomphe, France

Scenery taken during the trip while handling customer complaints

Eiffel Tower

Louvre

Palace of Versailles

LV flagship store

www.ingramcontent.com/pod-product-compliance
Lightning Source LLC
Chambersburg PA
CBHW041512210926
51847CB00011B/123